How I Memorized The Quran In 3 Years, And How You Can Too

Ibrahim Musa

Table of contents

Introduction

السلام عليكم ورحمة الله وبركاته

My name is Ibrahim. I currently live in the UK.

I have been sitting on the idea of writing this book for a while now, and I am glad that I am finally now taking the initiative to write it.

This book has been written in a way to help students from the west in their pursuit of the memorization of the Quran. That does not mean that this book will not be useful for you if you are not in the west; it just means that you may or may not relate to some of my personal experiences in my own journey of memorizing the Quran in London.

Alhamdulilah, I managed to memorize the Quran in 3 years, starting in June 2017 and finishing in June 2020.

The journey was by no stretch an easy one, and there were many ups and downs, a lot of distractions and tests from Allah. However, I am grateful for sticking by my schedule during difficult times, as it has now ultimately paid off.

Many people like to bring forth excuses as to why they cannot memorize the Quran, whether it be their age, their work circumstances or their lack of proficiency in the pronunciation of the Arabic letters.

Truth be told, I was not young when I started my journey, and likewise, I know many people personally who have memorized the Quran in their 30s and 40s. There is no doubt that the younger students tend to memorize better as they are less occupied and have a bigger capacity to absorb. However, it is without a doubt still possible regardless of your age. Many of the scholars of our time memorized the Quran in their late 20s, 30s and some even 40s. Don't let age stop you from embarking on this beautiful journey!

"I can't memorize because I work a full-time job!" is an excuse that we hear quite often. With good time management skills, you can certainly make time for an hour or two every day dedicated solely to the Quran. When I started my journey, I had just enrolled on a bachelor's degree course at university. I quickly realized that I needed to pick a time and stick by it every day. Like I always say, you will do something if you really want to, and you will make time for what you want to make time for.

"I don't know the Arabic letters" or "I have a bad pronunciation of the letters" is also an excuse which is often put forth. When I started, I knew the letters, but I could not read the mushaf very well.

I would stutter very often, and the speed I was reading at was very slow. If you don't know the letters or the Qa'ida, this can be learned in as little as a week or two. As for the pronunciation, this will also slowly come.

The more you immerse yourself in the Arabic Language and the recitation of the Quran, the easier this will become for you. This is also why it is absolutely imperative that you have a Qualified teacher whom you learn and recite to.

As parents, we all have a dream for our children to become huffadh and carriers of the Quran as we know the virtues of this noble act. However, don't you think that it is unfair to have this expectation of our children if we, at the very least, are not committed to our learning?

I am confident that by the end of this book, you will have a good idea of how to embark on this journey. The first chapter will be about the importance of setting your intentions before embarking on this journey. The second chapter will speak about the virtue of memorizing the Quran.

The third chapter will expand on the importance of learning from a qualified teacher. The fourth chapter will explain if it is necessary or not for a student to be fluent in the Arabic Language before starting. The fifth chapter is an important one, and one of the main reasons why a lot of people end up quitting halfway through their journey, it's on setting expectations and what is realistic or not. The sixth and final chapter will include all the memorization tips and techniques that I used personally and my daily routine.

The pieces of evidence in this book will be backed up by authentic ahadith and ayaat from the Quran.

Chapter 1: Why Do You Want To Memorize The Quran?

This is a question that we all ask ourselves before making that decision to start memorizing. The truth is that intentions are very important in Islam. This is because if we do an act of worship (Ibadah) other than to seek the reward of Allah, that action will not be accepted. At the same time, I have found that people can also use this as an excuse not to start their journey. Someone might say, "I don't know if my intentions are sincere", and use that to procrastinate and not start.

This chapter will speak on the importance of our intentions for all of our acts of worship, not just the memorization of the Quran.

Let's first start with the famous first Hadith in Sahih Bukhari.

عَنْ أَمِيرِ الْمُؤْمِنِينَ أَبِي حَفْصٍ عُمَرَ بْنِ الْخَطَّابِ رَضِيَ اللهُ عَنْهُ قَالَ
سَمِعْتُ رَسُولَ اللَّهِ صلى الله عليه وسلم يَقُولُ: إنَّمَا الْأَعْمَالُ بِالنِّيَّاتِ، وَإِنَّمَا لِكُلِّ
امْرِئٍ مَا نَوَى، فَمَنْ كَانَتْ هِجْرَتُهُ إلَى اللَّهِ وَرَسُولِهِ فَهِجْرَتُهُ إلَى اللَّهِ وَرَسُولِهِ،
وَمَنْ كَانَتْ هِجْرَتُهُ لِدُنْيَا يُصِيبُهَا أَوْ امْرَأَةٍ يَنْكِحُهَا فَهِجْرَتُهُ إلَى مَا هَاجَرَ إلَيْهِ

It is narrated on the authority of Amir al-Mu'minin (Leader of the Believers), Abu Hafs' Umar bin al-Khattab (may Allah be pleased with him), who said: I heard the Messenger of Allah (peace be upon him), say:

"Actions are according to intentions, and everyone will get what was intended. Whoever migrates with an intention for Allah and His messenger, the migration will be for the sake of Allah and his Messenger. And whoever migrates for worldly gain or to marry a woman, then his migration will be for the sake of whatever he migrated for."

The main thing that we need to take from this Hadith is that having the right intention is a fundamental part of a valid act of worship.
The great scholars of our time say that this Hadith is one of the four Hadith around which Islam revolves, showing us the great importance that Islam places on intentions when it comes to acts of worship, i.e. memorizing the Quran.

The first part of the Hadith, "inamaa", is a particle of restriction in the Arabic Language, meaning that it affirms the ruling of what comes after it and negates the ruling of what came before it.

The word "al amaal" (the actions) in this Hadith refers to the ibadaats ordained by Allah. As for the worldly actions, they do not require you to have an intention.

However, if you do a worldly action with the intention of that action helping you to worship Allah, you are rewarded for this deed. For example, sleeping within itself does not have a reward in it. However, if you sleep with the intention to wake up for Fajr prayer, you are rewarded for your sleep. The same is if you go to work with the intention of providing for your family, as it is a responsibility ordained by Allah upon the man, and you would also be rewarded for this.

You need to make sure that you are continuously renewing your intentions when you embark on the journey of memorizing the Quran. The salaf would fear hypocrisy and would renew their intentions every day. If you are doing this so you can get the "hafidh" or "hafidah" title, then you need to renew your intentions. Constantly make Dua that Allah purifies your intentions.

Chapter 2: The Virtues And Benefits Of Memorizing The Quran

Memorizing the Quran has many virtues. In this chapter, we will go over the ahadith related to the virtues of memorizing the Quran.

One of the greatest virtues of memorizing the Quran is that you are following in the footsteps of our beloved Prophet Muhammad SAW. As we know, the Prophet was illiterate. He did not know how to read or write. The Quran was revealed to him by Jibreel over the span of 23 years, meaning that whenever he would receive revelation, he would memorize what was sent down from his lord.

Also, while the Prophet was alive, there were many companions who had memorized the whole Quran from cover to cover, and they would teach it to others. The memorization of the Quran continued in different cities. For example, it continued in Damascus, Basra and Kufa.

Let us move on to some of the famous ahadith that display the virtue of memorizing the Quran.

عَنْ عَائِشَةَ عَنْ النَّبِيِّ صَلَّى اللَّهُ عَلَيْهِ وَسَلَّمَ قَالَ مَثَلُ الَّذِي يَقْرَأُ الْقُرْآنَ وَهُوَ حَافِظٌ لَهُ مَعَ السَّفَرَةِ الْكِرَامِ الْبَرَرَةِ وَمَثَلُ الَّذِي يَقْرَأُ وَهُوَ يَتَعَاهَدُهُ وَهُوَ عَلَيْهِ شَدِيدٌ فَلَهُ أَجْرَانِ

Aisha reported: The Prophet, peace and blessings be upon him, said, "The example of one who recites the Quran well and memorizes it will be in the company of the noble and obedient angels (80:15). The example of one who recites the Quran and is committed to it, although it is difficult for him, is that of one with a double reward."

This is a beautiful hadith because the Prophet tells us that a person who memorizes the Quran will be with the Angels in Jannah; who would not want to be with the angels in Jannah? The person who recites the Quran well or with proficiency is the one who is able to read according to the rules of ilm al tajweed.

Not only that, but this Hadith also gives hope to those who struggle with the recitation and the memorization of the Quran. The Prophet promised us that Allah would give you DOUBLE the reward of a person who does not struggle with the recitation of the Quran. Imam Bukhari explained that one reward is for the difficulty that a person encounters while reciting the Quran, and the other is for actually reciting the Quran.

Don't feel embarrassed to recite the Quran with your friends or family. Allah will reward you double-fold In Sha Allah.

Uthman ibn Affan narrated the famous Hadith of the Prophet, where he said:

وعن عثمان بن عفان رضي الله عنه قال: قال رسول الله صلى الله عليه وسلم
خيركم من تعلم القرآن وعلمه - رواه البخاري

The Messenger of Allah (ﷺ) said, "The best amongst you is the one who learns the Qur'an and teaches it."

This is a tremendous hadith, as it not only shows the excellence and importance of memorizing the Quran and implementing it but also teaching it once you are qualified to do so. We should all have aspirations that one day we will teach our children and family the Quran In Sha Allah.

We also know the famous Hadith of the Prophet SAW, where he said:

عَنْ مُعَاذٍ الْجُهَنِيِّ أَنَّ رَسُولَ اللهِ صَلَّى اللَّهُ عَلَيْهِ وَسَلَّمَ قَالَ مَنْ قَرَأَ الْقُرْآنَ وَعَمِلَ
بِمَا فِيهِ أُلْبِسَ وَالِدَاهُ تَاجًا يَوْمَ الْقِيَامَةِ ضَوْءُهُ أَحْسَنُ مِنْ ضَوْءِ الشَّمْسِ فِي بُيُوتِ
الدُّنْيَا لَوْ كَانَتْ فِيكُمْ فَمَا ظَنُّكُمْ بِالَّذِي عَمِلَ بِهَذَا

Mu'adh al-Juhani reported: The Messenger of Allah, peace and blessings be upon him, said, "Whoever recites the Quran and acts according to what is in it, his parents will be crowned on the Day of Resurrection with a light brighter than the light of the sun in your worldly houses, were it among you. What do you think of one who acts upon this?"

Do we not all wish that our parents were crowned on the day of resurrection? What a beautiful hadith this is. May Allah make us from those whose parents are crowned on the day of judgement because of our efforts with his book.

We also know the famous Hadith narrated by Abdullah ibn Amr:

عَنْ عَبْدِ اللَّهِ بْنِ عَمْرٍو عَنْ النَّبِيِّ صَلَّى اللَّهُ عَلَيْهِ وَسَلَّمَ قَالَ يُقَالُ لِصَاحِبِ الْقُرْآنِ اقْرَأْ وَارْتَقِ وَرَتِّلْ كَمَا كُنْتَ تُرَتِّلُ فِي الدُّنْيَا فَإِنَّ مَنْزِلَتَكَ عِنْدَ آخِرِ آيَةٍ تَقْرَأُ بِهَا

سنن الترمذي كتاب فضائل القرآن باب ما جاء فيمن قرأ حرفا من القرآن ماله من الأجر

Abdullah ibn Amr reported: The Prophet, peace and blessings be upon him, said, “It will be said to the companion of the Quran: Recite and ascend as you recited in the world. Verily, your rank is determined by the last verse you recite.”

What is actually meant by the companion of the Quran, though? The companion of the Quran is the one who has memorized it and has followed it to the best of his ability. We know from another hadith that the Prophet said:

عَنْ أَبِي مَسْعُودٍ الْأَنْصَارِيِّ قَالَ قَالَ رَسُولُ اللَّهِ صَلَّى اللَّهُ عَلَيْهِ وَسَلَّمَ يَؤُمُّ الْقَوْمَ أَقْرَؤُهُمْ لِكِتَابِ اللَّهِ

The one who knows the most Qur'an should lead the people in prayer

A person's status in Paradise will depend on how much Quran they memorized and recited in the Dunya; the more they memorized in this Dunya, the higher their status will be on the day of judgement, as long as their intentions are pure and for the sake of Allah.

We also know of another hadith of the prophet SAW:

عن أبي الْقَاسِمِ قال قال أبو أُمَامَة رضي الله عنه اقْرَءُوا الْقُرْآنَ لَا تَغُرَّنَّكُمْ هَذِهِ الْمَصَاحِفُ الْمُعَلَّقَةُ فَإِنَّ اللَّهَ لَا يُعَذِّبُ قَلْبًا وَعَى الْقُرْآنَ
مصنف ابن أبي شيبة

Abu al-Qasim reported: Abu Umamah, may Allah be pleased with him, said, "Recite the Quran and do not be deceived by depending on the written copies. Verily, Allah will never punish a heart that has memorized the Quran."

This is yet another beautiful hadith. The Prophet vowed that Allah would not punish a heart that has memorized the Quran as long as that person is sincere, stays away from sins and repents to Allah often

We also know of the famous Hadith of the Prophet SAW, where he said:

عن أبي أُمَامَةَ الْبَاهِلِي رضي الله عنه قَالَ سَمِعْتُ رَسُولَ اللهِ صَلَّى اللَّهُ عَلَيْهِ وَسَلَّمَ يَقُولُ: اقْرَءُوا الْقُرْآنَ فَإِنَّهُ يَأْتِي يَوْمَ الْقِيَامَةِ شَفِيعًا لأَصْحَابِهِ

Umamah (May Allah be pleased with him) reported: I heard the Messenger of Allah (ﷺ) saying, "Read the Qur'an, for it will come as an intercessor for its reciters on the Day of Resurrection."

When the scholars explained this Hadith, they said that this Hadith shows the excellence of the Quran and acting upon its rulings. The scholars explain that the Quran will be given the power of speech by Allah, and the Quran will ask Allah to forgive the sins of the people who recited and acted upon it, and Allah will accept this request.

Umar ibn al Khatab (May Allah be pleased with him) narrated the hadith of the prophet where he said:

وعن عمر بن الخطاب رضي الله عنه: أن النبي صلى الله عليه وسلم قال: إن الله يرفع بهذا الكتاب أقوامًا ويضع به آخرين رواه مسلم

'Umar bin Al-Khattab (May Allah be pleased with him) reported: The Prophet (PBUH) said, "Verily, Allah elevates some people with this Qur'an and abases others."

This Hadith again shows the importance of acting upon what we learn, as only those who acted upon Allah's commands and abstained from what he has made forbidden will rise. The scholars have explained that this does not only mean in the hereafter, no, they will be risen and have a high status in the worldly life as well, and vice versa; this also applies for the one who is abased by the Quran.

Ibn' Umar (May Allah be pleased with them) reported:

وعن ابن عمر رضي الله عنهما: عن النبي صلى الله عليه وسلم قال : لا حسد إلا في اثنتين: رجل آتاه الله القرآن، فهو يقوم به آناء الليل وآناء النهار، ورجل آتاه الله مالا، فهو ينفقه آناء الليل وآناء النهار- متفق عليه

The Prophet (ﷺ) said: "Envy is justified in regard to two types of persons only: a man whom Allah has given knowledge of the Qur'an, and so he recites it during the night and during the day; and a man whom Allah has given wealth and so he spends from it during the night and during the day."

As we know, you are not allowed to be envious of your Muslim brother/sister.

The scholars have commented on this Hadith, saying that Envy here actually means bliss, meaning that you wish for grace for your Muslim brother/sister and not Envy. The difference is that an envious person will want Allah to give you the blessing that the other person has and remove it from him/her, whereas a blissful person will want the blessing of the other person, but not at the expense of them losing it.

Let's now talk about some other benefits of memorizing the Quran that is maybe not discussed as much.

Benefit #1 – become a respected leader in your community

It is well recorded that when the Prophet SAW would assign roles of leadership amongst the sahaba, he would give preference to those who had memorized the most Quran. Not only this, but even in the west, Hufadh are generally regarded in a high esteem by their community, not that this should be your goal, but you will be honoured by the people and by Allah SWT.

We also know the famous hadith narrated by Abu Hurairah RA:

وعنه عن النبي، صلى الله عليه وسلم، قال: إذا أحب الله العبد نادى جبريل: إن الله تعالى يحب فلانًا، فأحببه، فيحبه جبريل، فينادي في أهل السماء: إن الله يحب فلانًا، فأحبوه، فيحبه أهل السماء، ثم يوضع له القبول في الأرض متفق عليه

The Prophet (ﷺ) said, "When Allah loves a slave, he calls out Jibril and says: 'I love so-and-so; so love him. Then Jibril loves him. After that, he (Jibril) announces to the inhabitants of the heavens that Allah loves so-and-so; so love him, and the inhabitants of the heavens (the angels) also love him and then make people on earth love him".

May Allah make us from those who he is pleased with and the people are also pleased with.

Benefit #2 Memorising improves neural plasticity

When you memorize the Quran, whichever technique you employ, there will be some sort of repetition involved. This is also known as rote learning. According to some Irish researchers, rote learning will improve your neural plasticity. This means that you will overall be able to recall information better, not just the Quran. I can 100% say that this is definitely the case. Memorizing the Quran really helped me with my secular studies. It made memorizing notes for my exams a ton easier, and I also found myself a lot more focused. This is all due to me learning how to focus when memorizing the Quran. I just shifted it to my secular studies.

Benefit #3 – the Quran is a cure

We know of the famous Hadith narrated by Abdullah ibn Masud:

عَنْ عَبْدِ االله بْنِ مَسْعُودٍ رضي االله عنهما قَالَ: فِي الْقُرْآنِ شِفَاءَانِ: الْقُرْآنُ وَالْعَسَلُ؛ القُرآنُ شِفَاءٌ لِمَا فِي الصُّدُورِ، وَالْعَسَلُ شِفَاءٌ مِنْ كُلِّ دَاءٍ. رواه البيهقي وقال: هذا هو الصحيح موقوف.

'Abdullāh Ibn Mas'ud said that he heard the Messenger of Allāh (peace and blessings of Allāh be upon him) saying: "There are two cures for you all: Honey and the Qur'ān.

Imam al bayhaqi commented on this Hadith. He said that the Quran is a cure for what is in the chests, and honey is a cure for every other disease.

We also know that there are certain sections of the Quran that we read when we are inflicted with something or when we do Ruqya (Islamic exorcism).

Benefit #4 – The Quran will soften your heart

People who have memorized the Quran are down-to-earth and kind people. The Quran will change your character and mannerisms with the people. Carriers of the Quran and very patient, kind and forgiving.

Chapter 3: Why You MUST Learn And Recite To A Teacher

What we have to understand is that the Quran is not like any other book on the face of this earth. This book is a revelation from Allah (God)

Allah tells us in Surah Muzammil:

أَوْ زِدْ عَلَيْهِ وَرَتِّلِ ٱلْقُرْءَانَ تَرْتِيلًا

According to ibn Katheer, He explains that according to imam Raghib, as explained in al-Mufradat, the word "tartil" means to put together and also arrange with proficiency the component parts of a word and speech, thus making it distinct. He explains that Quran must not be recited in haste, and instead, it should be recited in a well-measured tone.

This is one of the main reasons why you absolutely need a Quran teacher when embarking on this journey. A Qualified Quran teacher will teach you tajweed properly and will pick up any mistakes that you yourself might not realize when reciting to yourself.

No matter how proficient you think your tajweed is, there will always be something that you will be corrected on or something that you can improve on.

Another reason why you need a qualified teacher is that a teacher will not only teach you the Quran, but he will also teach you Islamic manners and cultivation. This is, of course, in an indirect way, but the more time that I spend with my teacher, the more I pick up his good traits and the closer that I feel to my creator.

As a parent, you should look for a teacher for your children that will not only teach your children the Quran but one that will also give them Islamic cultivation; he should be a role model for your children.

How to choose a good Quran teacher

There are a few things that you should look out for before choosing a Quran teacher that you will hopefully stick with for the duration of this journey.

The teacher should be fluent with his/her recitation

People often get this mixed up for the teacher needing to be a native Arabic speaker. Yes, while that would be ideal, however, you do not need to have a native Arab teacher. The most important thing is that the teacher recites with great proficiency, Tajweed and pronunciation of the letters.

I have seen fantastic Quran teachers that are very qualified. They are not native Arabs, so please do not make this a requirement for your Quran teacher because if you live in the west, the likelihood of finding a native Arab Quran teacher is slim anyway.

Having an Ijazah is desirable

An Ijazah is roughly translated in English as "Permission", "Authorization", or "license". When a teacher holds an ijazah, it authorizes him to teach and transmit a certain text or an Islamic field. The ijazah is bestowed by someone who possesses the Knowledge and authority in that field.

An Ijazah is very praiseworthy and important as it gives the student confidence that the teacher has the right qualifications to pass on this knowledge to his student. Think about it, could you become a lawyer in court without a law degree? The same applies to the Quran. The people who are qualified to teach are known by their ijazah.

Try to find a teacher who is knowledgeable in tafsir and other Islamic fields

Here in the UK, we pay a lot of attention to memorizing; unfortunately, though, little to no attention is paid to the tafsir (exegesis/ explanation) of the Quran.

We have to remember that the Quran was revealed for us to ponder over its verses. Allah says in Surah Saad:

"This is a blessed book which we have revealed to you (O Mohammad) So that they may contemplate its verses, and people of reason may be mindful.

How can we do tadabur (contemplation) over the verses of Allah if we do not understand them?

A Quran teacher should hopefully be fluent in the Arabic Language. They don't have to go over the tafsir of the whole Quran with you, as the memorization part will already take up a lot of time. However, they can teach you the tafsir of some of the surahs that we frequently recite in our Salah. There is no doubt that knowing the Tafseer of the surah you are reciting in your salah will increase your khushoo (your dignity and humility) in the prayer and draw you closer to your lord.

The teacher should have the correct Aqeedah (Creed)

This is the most important quality that you should look for in a teacher. Your Aqeedah (creed) is the foundation of your religion. You need to make sure that the teacher has the Aqeedah of Ahlus sunnah waljammah. Aqeedah is not just merely theoretical. Rather a person should implement what they have learned in Aqeedah in the form of action. This is also the reason why Ahlul sunnah wal jammah believe that Eeman consists of speaking with the tongue, believing in the heart and acting with your limbs.

In short, Aqeedah refers to the matters that a person believes in with certainty and conviction.

The word Aqeedah itself comes from the Arabic word عَقَدَ. This word is used to convey certainty and affirmation.

The matters of Aqeedah are those that Allah has commanded us to believe in. Allah says in surah al Baqarah:

ءَامَنَ ٱلرَّسُولُ بِمَآ أُنزِلَ إِلَيۡهِ مِن رَّبِّهِۦ وَٱلۡمُؤۡمِنُونَ ۚ كُلٌّ ءَامَنَ بِٱللَّهِ وَمَلَـٰٓئِكَتِهِۦ وَكُتُبِهِۦ وَرُسُلِهِۦ لَا نُفَرِّقُ بَيۡنَ أَحَدٖ مِّن رُّسُلِهِۦ ۚ وَقَالُواْ سَمِعۡنَا وَأَطَعۡنَا ۖ غُفۡرَانَكَ رَبَّنَا وَإِلَيۡكَ ٱلۡمَصِيرُ

"The messenger believes in what has been revealed to him from his lord, and so do the believers. They all believe in Allah, his angels, his books, and his messengers. They "proclaim: we make no distinction between any of his messengers", And they say "we hear and obey". We seek your forgiveness, our lord! And to you alone is the final return.

Therefore, in Islam, Aqeedah refers to the matters that are known from the Quran and authentic ahadith.

As you can now see, a person's Aqeedah is the foundation of a person's belief because everything builds from the Aqeedah. If a person's aqeedah is distorted, then everything else will be distorted.

Find a teacher who is known to hold onto the sunnah and one that takes from the scholars that are recognized to be on the correct methodology, both contemporary and the ones who have passed.

Where can I find a Quran teacher in the west?

Now that you know what qualities to look for in a good Quran teacher, it's important to know how you can come across such a teacher.

The first thing that you should do is to look locally and ask your local masjid (they should be upon the sunnah) if there are any Quran memorization classes ongoing at the moment. In most cases, you will find that there are always local classes ongoing, especially if you are in London.

Before I mention some of the online options at your disposal, it is important for a student to understand that they must be willing to make sacrifices if the right opportunity presents itself. For example, if you know there is a great Quran teacher in east London, and you are based in west London, you should strive and try your utmost best to make it to that teacher. Nowadays, we have public transport right at our fingertips. The Sahabas were unfortunately not as lucky. They had to travel for months on end on their riding beasts just for a single adahith.

We know the famous saying of imam Maalik: العلم يؤتى ولا يأتي

Which roughly translates to "Knowledge does not come to you. You have to go to it."

This saying shows us that we should strive to go to the bearers of Knowledge. They should not come to our doorstep to teach us.

Online options

There are so many online institutes where you can find teachers. I am personally not the biggest fan of online learning, especially when it comes to learning the Quran, but depending on where you are located, it may be your best option.

Some of the institutes that I am aware of and that I can recommend to you with conviction are:

https://www.madinahcollege.uk/ - Madinah college is based in Brixton, south London. They have extremely proficient teachers, some of which have an Ijazaah in the seven modes of recitation. Madinah college is also very affordable. It will cost you just £300 per year to recite to a teacher from the institute on a weekly basis. Each week you will get a 15-minute reading slot where you can recite the portion that you have memorized to a teacher. You also have a weekly tajweed class that ranges from 1-2 hours. I believe they have lessons on-site and online. Visit their website and see what works for you.

Imam shatibi institute https://shatibi.co.uk/ – this institute was established in 2010. This institute is based in the SW6 postcode in London, although they also have an online option as well. The price is on a month-to-month basis. It will cost you £50 a month for one 30-minute lesson a week.

One of the reasons why I am against the idea of learning the Quran online is that the teachers can sometimes find it hard to pick up your mistakes, which may be due to the bad internet connection or due to the volume/sound. I think you should only look for online options if you have tried everything to find something local. Not only will you be able to be corrected a lot easier in person, but you also pick up from the teacher's etiquette, and the relationship is a lot more personal. You can continue to build on it, whereas it is hard to do that online.

For the serious students

If you are serious about your Quran journey, I would highly recommend you to go to Egypt to learn. Egypt is known to be the best place on the planet to learn the Quran, they have very qualified teachers, and they are usually at a very low cost if you are coming from the west.

There are many institutes in Cairo and Alexandria where you can enrol and study. Some are free, while others are a small fee. Additionally, if you prefer the one-to-one setting more than the class setting, you can also find a teacher who can come to your flat every day, again, for a very good price. Finding one of these teachers is very easy, simply go to the masjid locally and ask for a local teacher. This usually works out very well. Just make sure to take into consideration the qualities that you should look for in a teacher.

Going to Egypt will no doubt come with its own trials as Egypt, and the eastern world, in general, is very different in terms of how things are done there, especially if this is the first time leaving your native country in the west. With that said, the benefits that you will pick up from studying in a country like Egypt will no doubt outweigh the difficulties that you might face.

Furthermore, you can also very easily study other Islamic sciences in Egypt to a high level; once you have grasped the Arabic Language and have memorized the Quran, you can very easily find a teacher to teach you the seven modes of recitation after your memorization of the Quran.

Chapter 4: Do I Have To Learn Arabic Before Starting?

This is a question that we hear a lot from students. What we have to remember is that the Arabic Language goes hand in hand with the Quran. Allah says in the Quran:

إِنَّآ أَنزَلْنَـٰهُ قُرْءَٰنًا عَرَبِيًّا لَّعَلَّكُمْ تَعْقِلُونَ

"Indeed, we have sent it down as an Arabic Quran so that you may understand."

We have to understand that a person cannot truly understand the beauty of the Quran until they have learned the Arabic Language. Yes, sure, there are plenty of translations of the Quran, but they are not the same. When you understand Arabic, you understand why certain verses were revealed and how they were revealed, you understand the grammar, and you are really able to soak in the beauty of the Quran.

People sometimes ask, "Why did Allah make the Quran in Arabic? Is it only for Arabs? Arabic is a hard language to understand."
Allah told us in the Surah Al Qamar:

وَلَقَدْ يَسَّرْنَا ٱلْقُرْءَانَ لِلذِّكْرِ فَهَلْ مِن مُّدَّكِرٍ

"And we have certainly made the Quran easy to remember. So, is there anyone who will remember?"

Ibn Kathir explains this verse in his Tafseer. He says that this verse means that Allah has made the Quran easy to recite for mankind upon the tongue. He has also made it easy to comprehend for those who seek to comprehend.

"So, is there anyone who will remember?"

Meaning is there anybody who will remember through this Quran, Which Allah has made easy to memorize and easy to understand. Allah also mentions in another verse:

فَإِنَّمَا يَسَّرْنَـهُ بِلَسَانِكَ لِتُبَشِّرَ بِهِ الْمُتَّقِينَ وَتُنْذِرَ بِهِ قَوْماً لُّدّاً

"So we have made this Quran easy in your own tongue (Arabic) so that you may give glad tidings to those who have Taqwa and warn with it the most quarrelsome people."

What we understand from these two verses is that Allah has made the Quran easy to understand and comprehend. Allah also chose Arabic as the Language of his book. Would Allah tell us that his book is easy to understand and comprehendible if the Arabic Language was really unattainable, as some people claim?

Absolutely not. Therefore, the Arabic Language is not difficult, and just about anybody can learn it with a bit of dedication.

We also know the famous statement of Umar Ibn Khataab (RA) where he said:

تعلموا العربية فإنها من دينكم، وتعلموا الفرائض فإنها من دينكم

"Learn Arabic as it is part of your religion and learn the obligations as they are also part of your religion."

There is no doubt that the Arabic Language is part of the religion, and anybody who wants to study the religion seriously absolutely has to learn the Arabic Language. There is only so much that can be translated into the English Language. As far as I know, only a small minority of the scholar's books have been translated into English. You would be missing out on a lot of Knowledge by just relying on the English Language.

Should I learn the Arabic Language first or memorize the Quran first?

This is a question that is very popular amongst students. A person should try their hardest to learn both at the same time. This is the ideal situation. However, because everyone has their own circumstances and situation, this may not always be possible.

In this case, you might have to pick one and dedicate your entire time to that subject only. There is no right or wrong answer to this. I will break down the pros of learning either one first. You can then decide which one you want to pursue.

The pros of learning Arabic before memorizing the Quran

Benefit #1 – you will memorize the Quran a lot quicker

This is a huge plus. You could potentially memorize the Quran in half the amount of time if you learn Arabic first. This is because once you learn Modern Standard Arabic to a good level, you will understand the Quran. Of course, you will still need to study Tafseer to know the context of the verses and reasons for revelation (سبب النزول). However, you will have a general understanding of the verses because of the amount of vocabulary that you have managed to acquire. When it comes to memorizing now, the words are familiar to you. They are not new, so your brain will pick up the verses a lot quicker, and they will be stored in your memory a lot quicker.

Compare this to someone who just about knows how to read the Quran. It will take them a lot longer to memorize. This is probably why I would learn Arabic first before I start memorizing the Quran.

Not only will you be able to memorize a lot quicker, but because you now have the Arabic Language, you essentially have keys to the whole religion. Meaning that you can study all of the other sciences in Arabic.

There is only so much that you can study in English, so this is a huge plus. You will be able to go directly to the scholars and take from them. There will be no need for a translator anymore at that stage.

In comparison, if you decided to memorize the Quran first with very little Arabic, you might end up completing the Quran in three or four years, but you would then have to spend another year or two learning Arabic anyway. So, if you learn Arabic first, in my opinion, you will also save a lot of time because you will memorize the Quran a lot faster.

Benefit #2 – You will understand the verses better and have more Ghushoo in your prayer

Another benefit of learning Arabic before memorizing the Quran is that you will understand the verses a lot better if you have already learned the Arabic Language. Compare this to someone who does not know the Language. He will have to constantly look at translations of the verses.

No doubt, understanding the verses will increase your Gushoo (humility) in prayer. How many times do we find ourselves in the tarawih prayer, wishing we understood what the verses meant that the imam is reciting? Now you will finally understand the verses. The feeling that you get when you understand the verses is one difficult to explain. You feel a lot more connected and tranquil.

Benefit #3 – If you wanted to go abroad and study in an Arab country, you could easily do so

Many students have a goal of memorizing the Quran in a country like Egypt due to the tremendous benefit that you get from the teachers there. What people would do is work for a whole year and save up money to come and study in Egypt for a full year. A lot of students during that year, though, won't do many studies, as they already have their minds on the following year, so they essentially waste that year.

If you plan to go to Egypt in a year and work to save up now, you can learn Arabic in your native country during that year. Yes, you can attain a very good understanding of the Arabic Language in just 12 months. You just have to be consistent and put in hard work and dedication.

If you spent that year in your native country learning Arabic, by the time you travel to Egypt to learn the Quran, you would have already grasped the Arabic Language to a good level, meaning that you can navigate through the country yourself, speak to teachers, get advice etc.

Most students who come to study in Egypt for the first time do not know the Arabic Language, so they rely on their network there to help them out and find a teacher for them. When you already know the Language, you can go and find the best teacher for yourself.

Pros of memorizing the Quran before learning Arabic

Pro #1 – It will open up doors for memorizing other Islamic texts very easily

This is a huge plus to memorizing the Quran first. When I finished the Quran, I was not necessarily very strong in Arabic (I am still learning, as we all are), but once you memorize such a large book like the Quran, I honestly believe you can go on to memorize almost any Islamic text. This is because your mind and brain are now used to memorizing at a large capacity, and you now know what it takes to memorize.

Let me give you a practical example. When I had memorized about five juz of the Quran, I tried to memorize some ahadith from imam Nawawis 40 ahadith, and I really struggled.

I tried the same thing when I finished my memorization, and it felt a lot easier. I assume this is because I had gotten so used to memorizing large portions of texts that it just felt very natural and easy to me.

Pro #2 – You will learn the Arabic Language quicker!

One of the pros of learning the Arabic Language first was that it would help you to memorize the Quran quicker. Well, the opposite can also be applied if you learnt the Quran first. This is because if you have already memorized the Quran, you have memorized a lot of Arabic words, which include verbs/ adjectives, nouns etc. So without you even knowing, you are already 35% there in terms of knowing Arabic. The only thing you would have to do from here is to solidify your understanding of the words that you have memorized from the Quran, but you don't have to memorize them again as you already have them memorized.

Pro #3 – it will give you a huge step when learning other Islamic sciences

We have to understand that the Quran and ahadith, as the Prophet and his companions understood them, are the foundations of our religion. No matter which field you want to study after the Quran, the Knowledge in those fields is derived from the Quran as the Quran is our criterion.

For example, if you wanted to study Aqeedah (Creed) after memorizing the Quran, you would be at an advantage compared to other students because you will come to realize that a lot of Aqeedah books like Thalathaul usool, Qawa'id al arbaa and Kitab al Tawheed are mostly made up of Quranic verses that are put into context and explained by the respective scholar. Because you already know the verses, you won't have to memorize them again, as the other students would have to do. You would simply need to understand the content of those verses in the field you are studying.

You could study a lot of material in the religion simply by memorizing the Quran, and it will give you a leg up over other students who have not memorized the Quran. Some scholars say that a person cannot be a student of Knowledge without memorizing the Quran. This shows us the importance of memorizing the Quran.

Now that I have given the pros of both, you should decide which one you want to pursue. Because this book is mainly targeted at students looking to memorize the Quran, I thought I would dedicate this small part of the chapter to explaining how a student would go about learning the Arabic Language from scratch.

How can I learn the Arabic Language from scratch?

As I have previously mentioned, it is very realistic to have a good understanding of the Arabic Language in as little as 12-16 months. The problem is that most people take the wrong approach.

They end up studying for years and years, seeing very little progress along the way.

If you are a complete beginner and you don't know the Arabic alphabet, the first thing you should do is learn the Arabic alphabet and the basic rules pertaining to it. You can learn this in about a week, and there are plenty of YouTube playlists that you can follow. Just make sure you type in "modern standard Arabic" and not any other dialect. Arabic has hundreds of dialects. As a beginner, you want to focus on modern standard Arabic, the Arabic that is widely recognized in the Arab world.

Once you have learned the alphabet, it's time for you to find a teacher or join an institute that will follow a conversational Arabic programme. The keyword here is conversational. Unfortunately, there is this trend in the west where institutes are obsessed with teaching the students grammar before they know how to construct a sentence in the Language.

Just think about it, when you learned English, did you start off with verbs and nouns? Or did you start off with small words, then broken sentences, and then you were able to speak properly? To this day, I don't know much English grammar, but I can speak it fluently. Unfortunately, it is very common that beginner Arabic students in the west to start learning this way.

I actually started learning Arabic through grammar myself, and I ended up wasting three years in the process. Let me briefly tell you my story.

I started with the famous Madinah books that are widely taught in the west. I completed all three books, each book is very thick, so it took me about two and a half to three years in total. At the end of the programme, yes, I became strong in nahu (grammar) and sarf (morphology). However, because the books were comprised of very little vocabulary, I could barely construct a sentence at the end of the programme. Every time I tried to pick up an Arabic book by one of the scholars, I couldn't pass the first line. As you can imagine, I was very frustrated, and I felt as if I had wasted three years of hard work.

Don't get me wrong, grammar and morphology definitely have an important role in the Arabic Language, and a person cannot truly appreciate the beauty of the Quran without learning grammar and morphology. With that said, I simply don't think it should be taught to beginner students who have no background or foundation in the Language. Once a person has sufficient vocabulary and can hold a conversation for a while, then it is the right time to teach them grammar and morphology.

It is said that for a person to be fluent in any language, they should know between 2000-3000 vocabulary words. For them to reach a native level, this would require 8000-10000 words.

This is only about 2% of the Arabic dictionary Lisaan Al Araab. This is very achievable, especially when you break it down into how many words you would memorize in a month, week and day.

After I had realized that I had learned the wrong way, I immediately researched alternative programmes that I could study that would allow me to learn and memorize a lot of vocabulary. I then came across the curriculum which is widely studied in Egypt called "Al Arabiya bayna yadayk" I briefly researched this programme and what other people had to say about it. All I read was positive, so I took the chance and started with book 1. Honestly, studying this series was the best decision I have ever made, and that is definitely not an exaggeration.

Just the first book had hundreds and hundreds of new words that I had not seen in any of the Madinah books that I spent years learning. The beauty of the bayna yadayk series is that it had plenty of conversations in the book where those words were being used, teaching us how to use them in context.

Another thing that I love about the bayna yadayk series is that it does have grammar, but it introduces just a little each chapter. In my opinion, it only teaches the students the basics of grammar and what they need to know at that stage in their journey. This is where I think the Madinah books lack. They have a lot of grammar rules that are very advanced, pretty pointless for the beginner as they don't need them right now.

At the end of book two of bayna yadayk, I could understand 80-90% of any Arabic video that I came across. I could pick up any Islamic book in Arabic and also understand a large portion of it. I am currently towards the end of book three, and I can honestly say that this is the best Arabic programme for any beginners who are serious about learning the Arabic Language.

You will learn a ton and ton of vocabulary and be able to apply that vocabulary properly, as long as you find a qualified teacher that can go over the curriculum with you. You can ask locally in your mosque if there are any ongoing classes that teach this series. I believe that it is starting to be taught a lot more now, especially in the UK. Do a simple google search of institutes near you that teach it, or if not, there are plenty of institutes that also teach it online.

Also, remember that Arabic is a huge ocean. As far as I know, Arabic has one of the largest dictionaries and vocabularies in the world. So, no matter how good you think you have become at the Language, there is always more to learn. Seeking Knowledge is not a two or three-year thing. We seek Knowledge for the entirety of our lives. As imam malik said:

أطلبوا العلم من المهد إلى اللحد

This roughly translates to "Seek knowledge from the cradle to the grave."

We also know the Hadith of the Prophet SAW, where he said:

عن أبي الدرداء -رضي الله عنه- عن النبي -صلى الله عليه وسلم- قال: مَنْ سَلَكَ طَرِيقا يَبْتَغي فيه عِلْما سَهَّل الله له طريقا إلى الجنة، وإنَّ الملائكة لَتَضَعُ أجْنِحَتها لطالب العلم رضًا بما يَصنَع، وإنَ العالم لَيَسْتَغْفِرُ له مَنْ في السماوات ومَنْ في الأرض حتى الحيتَانُ في الماء، وفضْلُ العالم على العَابِدِ كَفَضْلِ القمر على سائِرِ الكواكب، وإنَّ العلماء وَرَثَة الأنبياء، وإنَّ الأنبياء لم يُوَرِّثُوا دينارا ولا دِرْهَماً وإنما وَرَّثُوا العلم، فَمَنْ أَخَذَهُ أَخَذَ بحَظٍّ وَافِرٍ

Abu Ad-Dardā' (may Allah be pleased with him) reported: The Messenger of Allah (may Allah's peace and blessings be upon him) said: "Whoever follows a path in pursuit of Knowledge, Allah will facilitate for him a path to Paradise. Indeed, the angels lower their wings for the seeker of Knowledge of pleasure at what he does. Verily, the inhabitants of the heavens and the earth, even the fish in the water, ask forgiveness from Allah for the Knowledge. The superiority of a scholar over a devout worshiper is like the superiority of the moon over the rest of the stars. Indeed, the scholars are the inheritors of the prophets, who bequeath neither dinar nor dirham, only Knowledge whoever acquires it has actually taken abundant wealth."

Work hard, and as long as you don't give up, you will become fluent in the Arabic Language, In Sha Allah.

How Arabic helps you with the Quran

When you learn Arabic, not only will it help you to memorize the Quran from the standpoint of knowing what the verses mean, but it will also help you in terms of grammar.

When you know Arabic grammar, it is impossible to put the wrong vowels (Harakats) on the letters. Not only that, but you will also be able to end the verses correctly. For example, you will be able to differentiate if the verse is supposed to end with مجرمون or مجرمين. You will know that any noun after إنَّ will be mansub and take a fathah. These are all very Subtle but very important. I have observed that students who do not know the basic Arabic grammar to be making the most mistakes of this type.

These mistakes can range from very small to very big, and sometimes even haram. This is because if you put the wrong harakah on a word, it can completely change the meaning that Allah originally intended from that verse.

Let me give you an example. Allah says in the Quran:

إِنَّمَا يَخْشَى ٱللَّهَ مِنْ عِبَادِهِ ٱلْعُلَمَٰٓؤُاْ

"Only those of his servants who possess knowledge fear Allah."

As you can see in the verse, الله has a fathah. This is because it represents the object (also known as the مفعول به in Arabic) the object has to take a fathah in the Arabic Language. The object is the thing that the action is done upon. In this case, it is الله that is feared. On the other side of the verse, ٱلْعُلَمَـٰٓؤُا۟ takes a dammah. The reason why it takes a dammah is because it is the subject (or also known as the فاعل in Arabic), So it is the scholars/people who possess Knowledge (the subject) who fear the object, which is الله.

Now, if we were to switch those and say, for example:

إِنَّمَا يَخْشَى ٱللَّهُ مِنْ عِبَادِهِ ٱلْعُلَمَـٰٓؤَا۟

If you are a beginner, those two verses probably sounded identical to you, and you would not be able to differentiate between the meaning of the two. However, I have now completely changed the meaning of the verse ولعياذ بالله

Instead of it now saying "only those of his servants who possess knowledge fear Allah", the meaning of the verse now means "Allah only fears those who possess knowledge from his servants". As you can see, the meaning has completely changed, and this is very, very dangerous. This is no doubt haram, and if a person does this on purpose, they have committed كفر (disbelief), and this can take a person out of the fold of Islam.

This is just one example of the many examples in the Quran. As I said, something like this might slip your mind very easily. Unfortunately, this is very common, and this is yet another reason why a person should strive to learn the Arabic Language as well as memorize the Quran, so they can avoid making mistakes like this.

Other benefits of learning the Arabic Language

Outside of the benefits of learning the Arabic Language that is related to the deen, there are actually some other benefits that you may not be aware of.

Benefit #1 – Arabic opens up many doors for employment

There is no doubt that employers prefer candidates who have more languages. As Arabic is such a sought-after language for employers all over the world, you will put yourself in a good position when it comes to applying for work. You are also more likely to get work in the Arab world, which usually tends to pay a lot better than employers in the west.

Benefit #2 – Arabic is spoken in many different countries

Arabic is the official Language of over 20 countries. The Language is widely spoken. When you learn the Language, you will learn how to get your way around those countries.

If you came on holiday to one of the Arab countries or even decided to move to one of them in the future, you wouldn't have any problem fitting right in. And another advantage is that you would not be taken advantage of, especially in the marketplace. Unfortunately, many tourists get taken advantage of due to shop owners automatically assuming they are rich because they come from the west, not just in Arabic countries, but all over the world this happens.

Benefit #3 – Learning Arabic can help you learn other languages

Learning Arabic will help you to learn other languages such as Persian, Farsi, Turkish and a lot more. A majority of the lexicon that is used in these Languages are very similar or have the same root as Arabic words. The grammatical constrictions are also very similar.

Benefit #4 – We get an insight into Islamic heritage through learning the Arabic Language

Of course, we know that the Quran and Sunnah are in Arabic, but outside of those two, there is a huge rich Islamic heritage that has been left by some of the biggest minds worldwide. Learning Arabic gives us access to fourteen centuries of Islamic scholarship.

Benefit #5 – The Arab world is a great market for trade

As I have already mentioned, the Arab world has 22 countries. As a whole, the region is very lucrative for trade and business due to the GDP of $2.7 trillion.

There are many sectors and industries that have huge potential, some that are already thriving and growing year on year. These are the construction industry, finance, tourism, telecommunications etc. Also, since a lot of these Arab countries heavily rely on foreigners to continue pumping their economy, the opportunities will always be there if you are into business.

Chapter 5: How To Set The Right Expectations Before Starting To Memorize & Some Tips When Memorizing

Setting the right expectations before embarking on this journey is crucial. Yes, having high and lofty aspirations is admirable. However, you must also be realistic regarding the challenges that you will face during your journey. Let me tell you some of the main challenges that I faced.

Don't focus too much on when you want to finish the Quran. Rather, focus on HOW you will get there

While it is good to set targets and dates when we want to have the Quran memorized, I have found that a lot of students usually take this way too seriously. What ends up happening is that a student may set the goal of finishing his memorization in a year and a half or two years. During months 6-7, he might stop memorizing for a month due to a family emergency that may have occurred out of the blue. This same student might end up stopping in totally because of the huge emphasis that they placed on finishing the Quran in a set time period.

They have installed this mindset that if they do not finish in this time, they are a failure. This leads to them stressing themselves out with pressure and unrealistic short-term goals to reach the bigger picture.

Rather, yes, set a time span that you would like to finish the Quran in, but understand that, unfortunately, sometimes things are out of our control, and something may stop you from hitting your target. Once you accept that you may face a roadblock along the road, you immediately remove the pressure from yourself. Don't use this as an opportunity to be lazy and not hit your memorization goals. Rather see the Quran as a life mission and not a book that has a timer on it.

You will struggle to memorize at first

This is a big one, don't expect to go into it with a solid memory, especially if you have not memorized anything before. I remember when I first started, I would take an hour to memorize just a few Ayat's. Over time, my memory increased a lot, and I would be able to memorize a lot more at the same time. It can be demotivating and annoying at first because it can feel like you are spending all of this time and not getting much in return. Be patient, make dua to Allah and don't give up. Your memory needs to be trained for it to grow, just like any other muscle in your body.

You will surely hit your memorizing goals as long as you stick to a schedule, even if it takes a bit longer than you originally anticipated.

Don't rely on motivation to keep you going

This is another big one when we first start our memorization journey. We are all filled with excitement and motivation for one reason or another. This may be because you started with your friend or brother/sister or the general excitement you feel when embarking on such a journey. My biggest advice is that you should not rely on motivation to get you through these two/three years of motivation because, as with anything new that we start, we are highly motivated at first, but that motivation can come crumbling down very quickly for a variety of reasons. In the case of memorizing the Quran, you may start with a high rush of motivation, but after your first three months, you may feel unmotivated due to the little that you have memorized, even though you expected to have memorized a lot more at that stage. The goal is to be disciplined with your schedule and try to stick to it no matter what happens, motivation dies out, but discipline will always get you through.

There were plenty of times in my own journey when I simply did not want to memorize, we are all humans, and sometimes we just don't feel like memorizing on a day for whatever reason. I am very grateful that I still did memorize on those days. Had I relied on my motivation, I may not have finished the Quran.

Another thing that is closely linked to motivation is seeing the number of students in your class slowly decrease with time, don't let this make you feel unmotivated. When our class first started, we had about 60-70 students.

Towards the end, there were only eight students in the whole class. People will drop out, and the serious students will remain.

If you, for example, go to your memorization class with a friend, don't feel that you cannot come to class if your friend cannot come. No, still come by yourself, even if your friend ended up quitting the classes. Once you develop this sort of mindset, it will be very hard for anything to prevent you from hitting your goal in Sha Allah.

Things that prevent people from memorizing the Quran and how to overcome them

Students who struggle with Tajweed

This is a big one and one that I often see that discourages students from continuing. I especially see it with students with an Asian background, such as Pakistani, Indians and Sri Lankans. Some of the letters are very hard to pronounce for them. At this stage, they either continue to memorize wrong, or they simply stop due to the number of mistakes they are making.

Mastering the correct tajweed and pronunciation can be achieved by anyone, no matter where you are from. As a matter of fact, I know a few white revert brothers who are very proficient in their tajweed and pronunciation of the letters.

A good way to overcome this problem is to have a lot of patience and to find a teacher that is qualified that can help you with your tajweed and lack of pronunciation.

I recommend studying a tajweed book called Tuhfatul Atfaal متن تحفة الاطفال. The reason why this book is so good is that the book explains where each letter of the Arabic Language is omitted from your mouth, and with a qualified teacher, he will really be able to help you pronounce the letters properly.

Another good piece of advice I can suggest is reading out the letters you struggle with in Infront of a mirror, or recording them and listening back to the recordings, so you can see where you are going wrong, and your teacher could also further advise you.

Students who are inconsistent with attending their classes

This is probably the largest obstacle to students nailing down the memorization of the Quran, and this is something that I have seen first-hand with other students that were in my class. A student might come to class one week, not come for the next two weeks, then come again for two weeks, then miss another week. Such an inconsistent student will never memorize the Quran.

The Quran requires you to be serious and give it your absolute all. You need to cut out any distractions in your life that are wasting your time and not bringing you any closer to Allah and his religion.

I also find that students who are inconsistent like this never really last very long in the class, as the teacher will end up removing the student anyway. If you are one of these students, but you genuinely have a reason why you sometimes may not be able to make it to class, speak to your teacher and explain your situation to him.

Your teacher may be able to schedule a different day where only you can recite to him over the internet. This way, you are not missing out on any lessons but only re-scheduling them. This should only be your last resort, and a student should not turn to this if they don't have a good enough reason not to be turning up every week.

Students who memorize just before reciting to their teacher

Unfortunately, this is also quite common among students, especially students who only have to recite a page or two to the teacher on a weekly basis. I had to recite 5-6 pages a week to my teacher, so I had to make sure that my memorization was good and did not have leeway.

Don't memorize just before your lesson with your teacher. It may work in the short term, and you may recite fine on that day, but you are only fooling yourself because your memory of that surah will be very weak in the long term, especially if you are a student who slacks with their revision.

Not only that, but it is also very bad manners, and most teachers will pick up on it.

You have to honour your teacher and respect his time. Remember that Knowledge is travelled to and does not come to your doorstep.

A way to overcome this is to set a strict memorization schedule. More will be spoken about this in the coming chapters.

Some tips when starting to memorize

Tip #1 – Try to stick with the same Mushaf throughout your journey

You will find a lot of teachers and scholars who will also give you this same advice when starting to memorize. The reason that you want to try your best to keep the same mushaf throughout is that the script and the form of the verses, and where they are placed in the mushaf will leave an imprint in your mind when you are reciting the verses and looking at them on a frequent basis. Another thing to also consider is that the Quran comes in a few prints.

The image you see above is the indo-pack, south African print of the mushaf. This style is widely used in the Asian community.

This is the traditional Madinah script of the mushaf. I would say this one is the most commonly used one around the world. I personally prefer the Madinah script of the mushaf as the letters are clearer to me. However, whichever one you prefer, make sure that you pick a mushaf, and you try your best to preserve that same mushaf throughout your journey.

Tip #2 – try to start a class with a friend or a sibling/family member

When I started my journey 3/4 years ago, I started with my older brother. We would go to the classes together and come home together.

We would sometimes also revise together and recite to each other before we would recite to the teacher.

Try to find a friend or a family member who is also interested in embarking on this journey with you, you will keep each other motivated, and you can compete with each other in a healthy way, as Allah says in the Quran:

سَابِقُوٓاْ إِلَىٰ مَغۡفِرَةٖ مِّن رَّبِّكُمۡ وَجَنَّةٍ عَرۡضُهَا كَعَرۡضِ ٱلسَّمَآءِ وَٱلۡأَرۡضِ أُعِدَّتۡ لِلَّذِينَ ءَامَنُواْ بِٱللَّهِ وَرُسُلِهِۦۚ ذَٰلِكَ فَضۡلُ ٱللَّهِ يُؤۡتِيهِ مَن يَشَآءُۚ وَٱللَّهُ ذُو ٱلۡفَضۡلِ ٱلۡعَظِيمِ

"So compete with one another for forgiveness from your lord and a paradise as vast as the heavens and the earth, prepared for those who believe in Allah and his messengers. This is the favour of Allah. He grants it to whomever he wills. And Allah is the lord of the infinite bounty."

Allah also says in a similar verse:

وَسَارِعُوٓاْ إِلَىٰ مَغۡفِرَةٖ مِّن رَّبِّكُمۡ وَجَنَّةٍ عَرۡضُهَا ٱلسَّمَٰوَٰتُ وَٱلۡأَرۡضُ أُعِدَّتۡ لِلۡمُتَّقِينَ

"And march forth in the way (to) forgiveness from your lord, and for Paradise as wide as the heavens and the earth, prepared for those who have Taqwa."

Tip #3 Look out for Analogous verses – also known as "Mutashabihaat"

Mutashabihaat verses are verses that are very similar to each other. The two verses that I have listed to you above are examples of mutashabihaat ayaats, they are not necessarily the same, but they are very similar.

The deeper you get into your journey, the more you have to be aware of these verses and how to differentiate between them. Let me give you some more examples of mutashabihaat verses, so you have a good idea of what I mean:

وَقُلْنَا اهْبِطُوا بَعْضُكُمْ لِبَعْضٍ عَدُوٌّ وَلَكُمْ فِي الأَرْضِ مُسْتَقَرٌّ وَمَتَاعٌ إِلَى حِينٍ

The verse that is similar to this one is:

قَالَ اهْبِطُوا بَعْضُكُمْ لِبَعْضٍ عَدُوٌّ وَلَكُمْ فِي الأَرْضِ مُسْتَقَرٌّ وَمَتَاعٌ إِلَى حِينٍ

Another example is the verse:

وَ إِذَا لَقُواْ ٱلَّذِينَ ءَامَنُواْ قَالُوٓاْ ءَامَنَّا وَإِذَا خَلَوْاْ إِلَىٰ شَيَٰطِينِهِمْ قَالُوٓاْ إِنَّا مَعَكُمْ إِنَّمَا
نَحْنُ مُسْتَهْزِءُونَ

The verse that is similar to this reads:

وَإِذَا لَقُوا الَّذِينَ آمَنُوا قَالُوا آمَنَّا وَإِذَا خَلَا بَعْضُهُمْ إِلَى بَعْضٍ قَالُوا أَتُحَدِّثُونَهُمْ بِمَا
فَتَحَ اللَّهُ عَلَيْكُمْ لِيُحَاجُّوكُمْ

Another example is the verse:

وَأَخَذَ الَّذِينَ ظَلَمُوا الصَّيْحَةُ فَأَصْبَحُوا فِي دِيَارِهِمْ جَاثِمِينَ

The verse that is similar to this reads:

وَأَخَذَتِ الَّذِينَ ظَلَمُوا الصَّيْحَةُ فَأَصْبَحُوا فِي دِيَارِهِمْ جَاثِمِينَ

As you can see from the verses above, they all sound very similar, and to the untrained eye, it can look like the verses are all the same. This is not the case, and over time, the student will be able to differentiate between these similar verses with more practice and revision.

There is a great book out there titled "Verses with similar words in the noble Quran and how to distinguish between them" by Abdul Mohsen Bin Hamad Aleabbad Albadar.

I would not recommend that you pick this book up straight away because you don't want to confuse yourself. However, once you have completed half to three-quarters of the Quran, it is probably worth picking this book up and revising the verses that are very similar but different.

Tip #4 – Try to learn the meaning of the verses you are memorizing

Learning the meaning of the verses will dramatically help you with keeping the verses with you for a long period.

Learning the context of the verses also links with this point when you know the Tafseer and context of the surah. The Quran is arranged elliptically. This means that the verses often repeat themselves again and again. Learning the meaning of the verses alongside the repetition of certain key phrases, ideas or concepts will help you to strengthen your memory.

Tip #5 – Don't compare your progress to others

While it is very good to have a friend/relative that you attend classes with, it is important to know that you should not compare your progress with theirs. This is because we all memorize at different rates and with different techniques. Competing is healthy as long as your heart does not Envy. This is when it would become dangerous.

Tip #6 – Recite out loud when you are memorizing at home

This is one that I don't see discussed a lot, but one that is very important. Just as we advised before that you should pick a print and a mushaf and stick with it. The same applies here. When you recite to your teacher, you will be reciting out loud to a level where he/she can hear you clearly. Therefore it does not make sense to memorize in your head or recite very quietly. Rather, practise in a clear and loud manner, the same tone that you plan to recite to your teacher, so you get used to it and make as few mistakes as possible.

Tip #7 – Use the portions you have memorized in your prayer

This is an advice that I have heard from scholars. Some scholars say that a person should recite the surahs that he/she has memorized in the tahajud (night prayer). This will solidify their memory of that portion and allow them to gain khushoo in their prayer.

I would also highly recommend that you lead a few prayers at your masjid, maybe for Taraweeh. Again, this will solidify your memory as it puts you in a situation where you have to know the verses on the spot, so your brain will work extra harder to retain the verses in your head.

Tip #8 – Chose a distraction-free environment to memorize in

I can't stress enough the importance of memorizing in a distraction-free environment. I personally memorized in my bedroom while the door was shut. There was no TV, no tablets, no computers or any distractions. Where you memorize will either make or break your journey, and I literally mean that. Do not try to memorize in the living room, where there are lots of distractions and constant talking. If you share a room with a sibling and do not have the luxury of memorizing in your room, you can go to the masjid every day for an hour and memorize there, as the environment will be perfect.

Tip #9 – recite in a melodic tone

عن أبي لبابة بشير بن عبد المنذر -رضي الله عنه: أن النبي -صلى الله عليه وسلم- قال: مَن لَم يَتَغنَّ بِالقُرآنِ فَليسَ مِنَّا

Abu Lubābah Bashīr ibn 'Abd al-Mundhir (may Allah be pleased with him) reported that the Prophet (may Allah's peace and blessings be upon him) said: "Whoever does not recite the Qur'an with a melodious voice is not one of us."

As we can see from this Hadith, the Prophet SAW loved the Quran to be recited in a melodious and tranquil manner. Also, reciting with a melody is pleasing to one's ears. This provides you with the incentive to keep on memorizing.

You will also stay motivated when you realize that your melody is improving the more you practise.

Tip #10 – Use flashcards to remember certain verses

Some people are visual learners and remember better when flashcards are used. Perhaps you can write a verse that you are struggling with on a flashcard and bring it out multiple times during the day. It will help you to remember that verse. Just make sure you are connecting the verse with the one before and after it.

#Tip 11 – Teaching is a form of revision

You don't have to be a fully qualified student with an ijazah to teach members of your family or some close friends. If you have memorized a surah and recited it upon your teacher, it is a good idea to also teach it to some people close to you, or maybe your younger sibblings. Not only will you get rewarded as you will In sha Allah fall under the Hadith of the Prophet SAW, where he said: "The best amongst you is the one who learns the Qur'an and teaches it, but you will also solidify your memory of that surah.

Tip #11 – pick a Quran app and stick to it

For my memorization, I did the majority of it from my mushaf; however, there were some times when I would use the Quran app on my phone to memorize. Just as it is important to make sure you are using the same mushaf, I would definitely say the same about the app as well.

The reason for this is that all apps are different. Some of them have colours that represent tajweed. Others don't. Some of them have longer verses on each page, and you don't want this to confuse you as it may be different to your Mushaf, and some pages might appear to be longer, which can, of course, be problematic when connecting verses from one page to another. Try to keep things consistent and try to get an app that follows the same structure as your mushaf.

Tip #12 – have a daily "wird" of the Quran

Your daily wird is the portion of the Quran that you read outside of your memorization time. Your teacher will advise you that you should have a daily wird where you recite at least one juzz a day. This is not mandatory, but it is highly recommended. You can read your wird directly from your mushaf, and it should usually take about 20-30 minutes, depending on how fast you recite. It would be good to do the wird of the previous ajzaa that you have memorized from the Quran. For example, if you memorized juz amma and are now on juz tabarak, it would be a good idea to do a daily wird where you finish juz amma every day from Monday to Friday. If you do this consistently, you will be very strong in your memory, especially if you come towards the latter parts of the Quran, where the surahs get longer and longer.

Tip #13 – try to create your own rhythm of recitation

Creating your own rhythm does not mean that you have to become the next Mishary Al Alafaasy.

It doesn't even mean that you have to have the most beautiful voice. It simply means that you try to create a rhythm when you read the Quran that you later become known and recognized for. If you do not have your own rhythm, you can listen to your favourite reciter and try to create something that is similar but slightly different. Everyone has their own rhythm, how many breaths they like to take in between verses, their own unique voice and style etc. All of this sounds like it would not make a huge difference, however, once you get used to a certain rhythm, because a lot of the verses are very similar, you will find it a lot easier to pick up other verses over time with ease.

What I did a lot towards the end of my Hifdh journey was record myself. You don't need a microphone as you can do it directly from your smartphone. Listening back to your recitations will not only help you to pick out and continuous mistakes that you make, but it will also help you to develop your own rhythm. Once you get used to the sounds of your voice and what is possible with it, you will feel a lot more comfortable. Don't feel shy of your own voice. Your voice is beautiful in its own right, even if you don't think it to be.

Tip #14 – set the alarm for when it is time to memorize for the first month

This is a really good idea, especially if you are a person who is always busy and occupied with something. You can schedule a simple alarm on your smartphone every day for your allocated time for memorization.

Hopefully, after a month, you will get so used to it that you will not need it anymore. Just like a person who sets the alarm to wake up for work, after a certain period, his body becomes so used to waking up at that time that the alarm is no longer needed. Hopefully, the same will apply to your Quran.

Tip #15 – You have to sacrifice some of your leisure time

We have to realize that things that are worthwhile are not necessarily easy to get. They require a lot of sacrifices. The memorization of the Quran is by far the best type of tijarah (Business) that you can do with Allah.

Allah says in the Quran:

إِنَّ ٱلَّذِينَ يَتْلُونَ كِتَـٰبَ ٱللَّهِ وَأَقَامُوا۟ ٱلصَّلَوٰةَ وَأَنفَقُوا۟ مِمَّا رَزَقْنَـٰهُمْ سِرًّا وَعَلَانِيَةً يَرْجُونَ تِجَـٰرَةً لَّن تَبُورَ

"Surely those who recite the book of Allah, establish prayer, and donate from what we have provided for them, secretly and openly – can hope for an exchange that will never perish."

The exchange that will never perish in this verse refers to Jannah. Allah mentioned that those who recite his book, alongside the other things mentioned in verse, will have an eternal paradise.

Never think that you are spending too much time with the Quran in a day and that you could be doing other things. The Quran is the best investment that you can make with your time. We know the famous Hadith of the Prophet SAW, where he said:

مَنْ قَرَأَ حَرْفًا مِنْ كِتَابِ اللَّهِ فَلَهُ بِهِ حَسَنَةٌ وَالْحَسَنَةُ بِعَشْرِ أَمْثَالِهَا لاَ أَقُولُ الم
حَرْفٌ وَلَكِنْ أَلِفٌ حَرْفٌ وَلاَمٌ حَرْفٌ وَمِيمٌ حَرْفٌ

Ibn Mas'ud (RA) said: "Whoever recites a letter from the Book of Allah, he will be credited with a good deed, and a good deed gets a ten-fold reward. I do not say that Alif-Lam-Mim is one letter, but Alif is a letter, Lam is a letter, and Mim is a letter."

This Hadith shows us the tremendous rewards that we can rack up from reading the Quran. A simple recitation of Alif-Laam-Meem is 30 rewards. Reciting a whole page of the Quran does not take us longer than 3-4 minutes, yet look at how many rewards we get from doing so.

There will be times during the weekend or even weekdays when you may feel like going out with your friends to eat or do something with your family. I'm not telling you to say no each time; however, you have to try and maximize the amount of time that you spend with the book of Allah, try to cut out any time that takes you away from your memorization, and especially your revision of that portion.

Tip #16 – Don't move on to another surah until you have memorized the current one

This is a big one. A lot of students often get hasty when it comes to memorizing the Quran, especially when they have a few more juz left.

Being hasty when memorizing is one of the biggest mistakes you can make because you will have to spend that time and more time later on to strengthen your memorization of that surah. Students who rush their memorization of a surah the first time will more often than not have a hard time storing that surah in their long-term memory. Whereas, if you just spent a bit longer on that surah, but you memorized it well, it will be like Fatihah later on, and even if you don't recite it for a few days or weeks, I have found that it will come back to you quickly. This is the benefit of memorizing properly the first time round.

Tip #17 – Take advantage of your age!

If you are reading this book and you are still relevantly young, you should take advantage of your youth. The "golden years" of memorization are from the ages of five to twenty-three. Not to say that you cannot memorize after the age of twenty-three. You absolutely can, but once you get older, memorization is not as easy for you anymore.

This can be for a variety of reasons, such as general responsibilities, you may be married and have less time, you may be working a job etc. There is a famous saying in Arabic that says:

اَلحِفْظُ فِى الصِّغَرِ كَالنَّقْشِ عَلَى الْحَجَرِ وَ الْحِفْظُ فِى الْكِبَرِ كَالْكِتَابَةِ عَلَى الْمَاءِ

"Memorizing in childhood is like engraving on a stone while memorizing at an old age is like writing on water."

Engraving a stone is an easy task, but writing on water is impossible. Again, not to say that it is not possible to memorize at an older age, but it will be more difficult. This is why we see many parents who get their children to memorize the Quran at a very young age, sometimes seven, eight and nine years old. They say that a person this young lacks understanding. However, his/her ability to memorize is very good. Therefore, even though you may feel that your children do not understand anything of the Quran, you should still cultivate them to memorize it at such a young age. A lot of parents don't like the idea of their children memorizing at such a young age due to their lack of understanding. This is surely a whisper from the whispers of Shaytaan. They may not understand now, but when they reach an age of understanding (usually in their late teens), it will be a lot easier for them, as they will already have the Quran memorized, compared to a parent who only encourages his child to start memorizing when they feel like they can understand what they memorize. Don't waste your child's greatest years of memorization!

Tip #18 – Your success is from Allah only

We have to understand that any success we have in the Dunya and deen comes from Allah, and Allah only. Allah tells us in the Quran:

وَمَا تَوْفِيقِي إِلاَّ بِاللهِ عَلَيْهِ تَوَكَّلْتُ وَإِلَيْهِ أُنِيب

"And my success is not but through Allah. Upon him, I have relied, and to him, I return."

This is such a powerful verse because it immediately makes you bury any arrogance that you may have in your heart. Attributing any success that you may get in this dunyah to Allah is the way of a true Muslim. Allah also tells us in Surah Ibrahim:

وَإِذْ تَأَذَّنَ رَبُّكُمْ لَئِن شَكَرْتُمْ لَأَزِيدَنَّكُمْ ۖ وَلَئِن كَفَرْتُمْ إِنَّ عَذَابِى لَشَدِيدٌ

"And remember when your lord proclaimed, 'if you are grateful, I will certainly give you more. But if you are ungrateful, surely my punishment is severe."

Be grateful for any achievements in your life, no matter how big, or small they are, and always attribute your success to Allah, so he can increase you more in goodness.

Tip #19 – Fight through the tough periods

There will be many periods when you will not feel like memorizing or revising your Quran. You have to strive hards against your soul, no doubt it will be difficult, but it will be worth it in the end. Had I not fought through my difficult periods, I am sure that I wouldn't have memorized the Quran. Alhamdulilah, Allah gave me the tawfeeq to push through. Tie your camel and make dua to Allah that he pushes you through difficult periods.

If you are going through an Imaan crisis, surround yourself with good companionship. We know the Hadith of the Prophet SAW, where he said:

حديث أبي هريرة : أن النبيِ ﷺ قال: الرجل على دين خليله، فلينظر أحدكم من يخالل

"A man is on the religion of his close companion, so watch you take as a close companion."

We often times underestimate the effects that our friends have on us. You are literally a reflection of your best friend, and more often than not, you will pick up their characteristics and traits, and vice versa. Don't befriend people who have completely different goals to you and friends that are indulged in haram. I am not saying that you should completely cut them off, no. Call them to the way of Islam with hikmah, as Allah says in the Quran:

ٱدْعُ إِلَىٰ سَبِيلِ رَبِّكَ بِٱلْحِكْمَةِ وَٱلْمَوْعِظَةِ ٱلْحَسَنَةِ ۖ وَجَٰدِلْهُم بِٱلَّتِى هِىَ أَحْسَنُ

"Invite to the way of your lord with wisdom and kind advice, and only debate with them in the best manner."

So yes, call your friends to the right path with wisdom and in a kind manner, but that is not to say that you should let them drag you to their misguidance and ultimately into the hellfire. This is why you should befriend someone who is on the same journey as you. Not only will you be able to keep each other motivated, but you will also be around good company that will always remind you of Allah and keep your Imaan high.

Tip #20 – Avoid sins as much as possible

Sins are a huge reason that may prevent a person from flourishing in his deen or in the dunyah. Allah told us in the Quran:

وَمَا أَصَابَكُم مِّن مُّصِيبَةٍ فَبِمَا كَسَبَتْ أَيْدِيكُمْ وَيَعْفُو عَن كَثِيرٍ

"And whatever affliction befalls you is because of what your own hands have put forth, and he pardons much."

When ibn Kathir was explaining this verse, he said that whatever infliction that has happened in your life is because of a sin that you have committed.

In the second part of the verse, where Allah says, "and he pardons much", Ibn Kathir says that no matter how many sins you commit (minor sins), he pardons you for it and does not punish you (As long as you come with sincere repentance)

Allah also told us in another verse:

ظَهَرَ ٱلْفَسَادُ فِى ٱلْبَرِّ وَٱلْبَحْرِ بِمَا كَسَبَتْ أَيْدِى ٱلنَّاسِ لِيُذِيقَهُم بَعْضَ ٱلَّذِى عَمِلُوا۟ لَعَلَّهُمْ يَرْجِعُونَ

"Corruption has spread on land and sea as a result of what people's hands have done so that Allah causes them to taste the consequences of their deeds and perhaps, they might return to the right path."

When Ibn Kathir commented on this verse, he said that the shortfall of crops and fruits was due to what people's hands had done.

"So that Allah causes them to taste the consequences of their deeds and perhaps they might return to the right path," Ibn Kathir said that Allah may trial a nation with loss of wealth, souls and fruits as a form of punishment, and so that they can make sincere repentance to Allah and come back from their sins.

We also know the famous Hadith of the Prophet, where he said:

عن أنس بن مالك رضي الله عنه قال: قال رسول الله صلى الله عليه وسلم: كلُّ بني آدم خَطَّاءٌ، وخيرُ الخَطَّائِينَ التوابون

Anas ibn Mālik (may Allah be pleased with him) reported that the Prophet (may Allah's peace and blessings be upon him) said: "All human beings are sinners, and the best of the sinners are the frequent repenters."

This Hadith shows us that we all make mistakes and we are all going to sin. If that was not the case, then Allah would not have created us in the first place. What we have to remember is that we should repent as soon as possible when we commit a sin. Allah says in another verse:

وَلَوْ يُؤَاخِذُ ٱللَّهُ ٱلنَّاسَ بِمَا كَسَبُواْ مَا تَرَكَ عَلَىٰ ظَهْرِهَا مِن دَآبَّةٍ

"And if Allah were to punish people immediately for what they have committed, he would not have left a single being on earth."

Sa'ad ibn jubayr said, commenting on this verse: If Allah was to punish the people for all of the sins they committed, he would have destroyed people's livestock and crops, and there would not have been a single moving creature on this earth. But Allah is delaying it until the day of judgement.

One of the benefits of Allah delaying sins until the day of judgement is that Allah gives us time to repent for those sins. We know the famous Hadith of the Prophet, where he said:

عَنْ أَبِي أُمَامَةَ عَنْ رَسُولِ اللهِ صَلَّى اللهُ عَلَيْهِ وَسَلَّمَ قَالَ إِنَّ صَاحِبَ الشِّمَالِ لِيَرْفَعُ الْقَلَمَ سِتَّ سَاعَاتٍ عَنِ الْعَبْدِ الْمُسْلِمِ الْمُخْطِئِ أَوِ الْمُسِيءِ فَإِنْ نَدِمَ وَاسْتَغْفَرَ اللهَ مِنْهَا أَلْقَاهَا وَإِلَّا كُتِبَتْ وَاحِدَةً

Abu Umamah reported: The Messenger of Allah, peace and blessings be upon him, said, "

Verily, the angel on the left side will raise his pen over the error or sin of a Muslim servant for six hours. If he sincerely regrets it and seeks forgiveness from Allah, the angel will throw it aside. Otherwise, he will record it as one sin."

Subhanallah! This Hadith is tremendous. This Hadith shows us the mercy of our lord. He gives his servant 6 hours to repent from a sin after it has been committed. If he repents, then the sin will not be written, but if he does not, he will only write it as one sin.

On the other hand, we know that if we do a good deed, we get ten rewards for it. Allah says in another verse:

مَن جَآءَ بِٱلْحَسَنَةِ فَلَهُۥ عَشْرُ أَمْثَالِهَا ۖ وَمَن جَآءَ بِٱلسَّيِّئَةِ فَلَا يُجْزَىٰٓ إِلَّا مِثْلَهَا وَهُمْ لَا يُظْلَمُونَ

"Whoever comes with a good deed will be rewarded tenfold. But whoever comes with a bad deed will be punished for only one, and none will be wronged."

This verse again shows us the mercy of our lord. Hasten towards the mercy of your lord, O son of Adam!

Chapter 6: Practical Tips And Strategies To Memorise The Quran

I know this is the chapter you have been waiting for. Everybody thinks that there is some sort of secret memorisation trick that helps people to memorise, but this is certainly not the case, although I will tell you what I did exactly to memorise the Quran within three years and how to maintain it to a good level after as well.

I want to break this chapter into a few practical steps. They are:

- Choosing your schedule – how many times a week are you going to memorise, and for how long?
- How are you going to memorise it? What is the memorisation technique that you will use?
- Which reciters shall I listen to while memorising?
- What will your revision strategy be?
- How much will I recite to my teacher on a weekly basis?

Choose your schedule and stick by it!

You should choose a schedule before you even start memorising. Don't start memorising without picking a time that you will stick with every day, no matter what happens. If you don't take the schedule seriously, you will most likely not take your memorisation seriously.

Whereas, if you slowly program your brain that a certain portion of the day is for Quran and Quran only, you will likely stick by the schedule.

Making a memorisation schedule will differ from person to person because we all have different responsibilities. Some of us may be working a full-time job, some may be at college or university, and others may be working a part-time job.

I had just started my first year in university when I decided that I wanted to take memorisation seriously. As a full-time university student, I had lectures three/four times a week. I was off for the rest of the days. Due to the fact that my university lectures started early afternoons on most days, I would finish my university day quite late and get back home around 6-7 pm.

This then allowed me to decide that I wanted to memorise during the evening, as that worked out best for my schedule, and it would also give me enough time to get home, shower, have dinner, pray and then start memorising.

This is just an example of what my schedule was, although what worked for me will not necessarily work well for you. If you work a full-time 9-5 job, doing one hour of memorisation in the morning after fajr might be a better option for you, especially if you are married, have kids and have responsibilities.

If you are a college/high school student who goes to school between the hours of 9-3, you have more options than a full-time worker and university student. There is no fixed time that a person should choose as each person's situation is different. However, what I would definitely say is that memorising Quran in the morning after fajr has virtues over any other time in the day.

The evidence for this is the hadith of our beloved prophet Muhammad SAW. It was narrated from Sakhr Al-Ghamidi that the messenger of Allah said:

اللَّهُمَّ بَارِكْ لأُمَّتِي فِي بُكُورِهَا

"O Allah, Bless my nation in their mornings (i.e. what they do early in the morning)

As we can see from this hadith, there is tremendous virtue in doing ibadaat (Acts of worship) in the morning.

How many days a week should you memorise?

Well, if you want to memorise the Quran in 2-3 years, you will need to memorise five pages a week, and that would be equal to a page a day.

Let's break the numbers down for you. There are 604 pages in the Quran. If you memorise five pages a week, you should expect to memorise the Quran in two years and two months. Of course, if you are just starting out and have just learned how to read, this is not a realistic expectation. I remember when I just learned how to read, I would start with a quarter of a page, then maybe 2-3 weeks later move to half a page, then one month later I would move to a page a day.

If you memorise four pages a week, you will memorise the Quran in close to three years. This might be a more realistic option for you. I would say that I took roughly three years because when I started, I did not start with the intention that I would finish in two or three years; therefore, the first 3-4 months were not seriously planned, nor did I follow a strict schedule per say, however, when I realised that I had memorised two juzz and that I had potential to finish the Quran, this is when I set a schedule and followed it, no matter what! I think this was a mistake that I made. Not taking the memorisation of the Quran serious from the start cost me six more months of memorisation. I have no doubt that had I started with a serious approach from the start. I would have finished at least six months before I actually did.

What you should learn from this is the importance of setting a timetable and sticking to it. Because we are breaking down the numbers, the only thing that will prevent us from hitting our objectives is becoming lazy.

Therefore, we put ourselves in a position where we have to hold ourselves accountable because we calculated the numbers, and we know what is possible and realistic.

Memorisation, like any other skill, improves the more you practice and exercise your brain. At first, you will likely struggle because the language is likely new to you, and you haven't memorised anything of this substance before. This is totally normal, and you shouldn't be disheartened if this happens to you. The important thing is to stick to your timetable and schedule because if you do, it will no doubt pay off in the long term.

However much you decide to memorise in a week, make sure that you set realistic expectations that you know you can follow. As Allah says in the Quran:

بَلِ الْإِنسَانُ عَلَىٰ نَفْسِهِ بَصِيرَةٌ

"Mankind is well informed about himself"

You know what you can bear and what you cannot. Pick a number of pages that you know you can maintain throughout the year, even if it is just 1 page a week. It might mean that you will finish later than everybody else, but at least you will eventually finish in sha Allah. If you set a target of 10 pages a week, even though you know that you would not be able to do that, you will likely never finish because you will probably give up a month or two into your journey.

Remember that slow progress is better than no progress.

How much time shall I spend memorising?

How much time you spend memorising will depend again on your schedule and how much time you are willing to sacrifice doing things you would usually do. I figured that one hour a day, Monday to Friday, worked best for me. The one hour would include spending about 10-15 minutes revising what I memorised the previous day and then moving on to new memory.

I believe that one hour a day is totally possible for most people, regardless if you are a full-time worker or a university student. If we add up all the time that we waste during the week, you will be surprised at how many hours we waste unknowingly. You can go to your iPhone settings, go on the screen time. You can view it by a week or by day.

Once you see your screen time and how many minutes/hours you waste on social media or on your phone in general, work to slowly cut that lower and lower every week. Within due time, you will find yourself having a lot more time than you originally anticipated. The biggest problem with people who claim to not have any time to memorise the book of Allah is that they are unwilling to sacrifice some of their own leisure time or time they spend with friends and family. We all have a tendency to waste time, but once you can control where you spend your time, you will find yourself having more than enough time for the Quran every day.

If you are a person who is easily distracted by your phone, try to limit your use by simply switching off your phone during times of the day and during memorisation. Invest in one of those boxes where you can lock up your phone for a period of time so you do not get the urge to constantly reach for your phone. Perhaps put your phone in aeroplane mode during the time of memorisation, so nobody can call or message you. There are lots of initiatives that you can take to dramatically increase your free time. At the end of the day, it comes down to how badly a student wants to memorise the book of Allah and the extents they are willing to go to reach their goal.

Which reciters shall I listen to while memorising?

Even though we have already discussed the importance of a teacher when embarking on this journey, you will only go to recite to your teacher during some part of the week, which means that the majority of the time you will be at home memorising, your teacher will correct you when you recite to him, but he/she is not present when you memorise. For this reason, it is absolutely crucial that you memorise while listening to the recitation of the surah you are memorising. I used to do it verse by verse. Meaning that I would play one verse, memorise it and then move on. I would only move on once I had memorised the first verse.

I would highly recommend you listen to sheikh Mahmoud Khalil-Al hussary and sheikh Muhammad Siddiq Al Minshawi while you are memorising.

This is because they recite with almost perfect tajweed, and they recite at a slow pace, meaning you can keep up with them, unlike some of the more fast-paced reciters nowadays. If you listen to either of these two sheikhs when you are memorising, and you imitate their pronunciation of the letters and tajweed as best as you can, you will, In Sha Allah, have only a few mistakes when you recite your weekly portion to your teacher.

A student who does not listen to any reciters while memorising at home and attempts to memorise the verses based on his understanding of tajweed will mostly end up a disaster, especially if a person is a beginner. Therefore, it is important to both have a qualified teacher while memorising but also to listen to a slow-paced reciter when memorising, so you minimise the number of mistakes that you will make.

How much will I recite to my teacher on a weekly basis?

This will depend on a few factors such as how many lessons you have with your teacher a week, and also how much capacity you have to memorise.

I only had one lesson a week with my teacher in class, and because I was memorising five pages a week from Monday to Friday, I would recite all five pages in our lesson on Saturday. At first, however, I started with only memorising half a page a day, and therefore I would recite 2.5 pages a week to my teacher.

This number will also differ if you attend class more than once a week.

I know a lot of students who attend a class every day from Monday to Friday. If this is the case, and you are memorising a page a day, then you would recite the page you have memorised the previous day. For example, on Monday morning, you would recite the page you memorised on Friday. On Tuesday, you would recite the page you memorised on Monday. If you don't want to recite pages that you memorised from the previous week, you could recite two pages on one of the days in the week to make up for it, the choice is yours, and it all really depends on what you are comfortable with.

Speak to your teacher to decide your recitation schedule with him/her. Some teachers prefer to listen to smaller portions, and others don't mind listening to you for twenty pages long. It also depends on the number of students in your class and how long the class is going on. You don't want to overburden your teacher. Make it easy for him/her.

Quran revision strategy

I cannot stress on the importance of constantly revising the portions that you have memorised of the Quran. Many teachers actually tell you that memorising itself is not the hard part, but the hard part is retaining what you have memorised. Once I finished my own personal journey, I could not agree more with this.

We often found that the students who took their revision seriously were those who retained their Quran the best.

I will personally tell you my own revision strategy. Feel free to take it for yourself or modify it how you see fit.
As I said, I would memorise a page a day for five days a week. The reason why it was not seven days a week is that you need the two days on the weekend to revise everything that you were memorising during that week.

There are two stages to my revision strategy when memorising:

The first I have already briefly mentioned, this is the start of every new memorisation day. Let's say I memorise a page of Surah Al Baqarah on Monday. On Tuesday, I would, of course, memorise the next page. However, before I do that, as I said, I take out 10-15 minutes to revise the previous page that I had memorised the day before. You will find that the first time you memorise a portion, it will appear to you that it is stored in your strong memory, but this is not the case at all. The next morning when you wake up, your memory of that page that you memorised becomes very blurry and weak.

This is something that puts off a lot of students because they think that they have a problem with their memory or they did not memorise properly.

No, this is not the case. It is normal for you to wake up and have weak memorisation of the page you memorised the previous day. It is important, though, that you revise that page again the next day.

As I already said, I would spend roughly an hour a day on my memorisation (10 minutes of those would be revising the previous page); however, I would also spend another 20-30 minutes during the day revising the previous page I just memorised. I usually did this when I would be commuting to university by train. I would constantly go over the previous page that I had memorised the day before. The 20-30 minutes sounds like a short period of time, and a person wouldn't expect it to make a big difference but trust me, it will absolutely solidify your memorisation of that page.

This, alongside the 10 minutes I take out before each fresh sitting, dramatically helps me to store the page in my long-term memory. I would only be able to do 20-30 minutes outside of the hour of memorising, but if you can do more, I would definitely recommend that you do take that opportunity if you can, as it will only make your life easier when you become a haffidh.

Again, to re-cap this revision strategy, let's say, for example, I memorised the first page of Surah al Baqarah on Monday, on Tuesday morning, or during my commute to university, I would revise the page I memorised on Monday for 20-30 minutes.

Then again, at 7-8 pm, when I get home, I would revise that page again for 10-15 minutes before I move on to the next page of memorisation. During this period, you would have revised the first page about 5-10 times before you move on to the next page. This will again help to solidify the memorisation of this page.

On Saturday and Sunday, my routine will greatly differ because on the weekends, we don't memorise anything new. What I do on Saturday and Sunday is a one-hour revision session on Saturday and also one on Sunday.

I will do this all the way from Monday-Friday.

What I try to do during the one-hour revision session on both days is to repeat every page that I memorised during that week at least 3-5 times. In total, I would have read at least 15 pages in that one hour. This will again solidify our memory for those pages and allow them to be stored in our long-term memory.

Please do not try to memorise seven days a week, yes, you may end up memorising more, but you will really struggle to retain what you have memorised, and because you are memorising every day, you will not have a lot of time to revise what you memorised anyway.

I know other students who did one day of revision and six days of memorisation. I personally think that five days of memorisation and two days of revision worked out well for me because it gave me more than enough time to revise everything that I learned while also taking that little break during the weekend from memorising. Remember, we want to stay motivated during our journeys and not quit. I find that memorising five days and revising two days gives me a great balance and enough time to rest up and recoup energy for the next week.

Memorisation techniques

I suspect this is the part you have been most eager to read. I will explain the memorisation technique that worked well for me, but I must say that whatever worked for me will not necessarily work for you. We are all different in how we learn and absorb information. I will explain my technique with examples, and I will also explain some other memorisation techniques that worked well for other students. I would recommend that you try a bit of all of them and see what works best for you. It is important that once you have your memorisation technique/style, you stick with it. This is because you will get used to a specific rhythm and the way in which you take in the verses. You don't want to disturb that by constantly changing it.

My memorisation technique

Okay, let's say, for example, we are memorising the first page of surah Mulk.

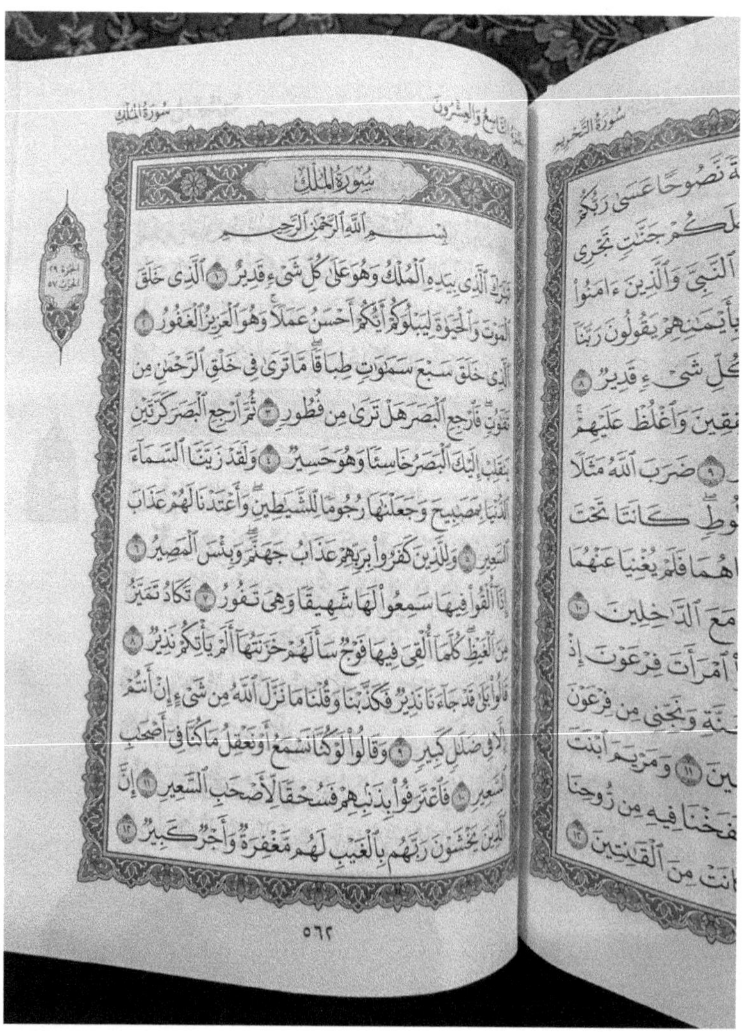

الجزء التاسع والعشرون — سورة الملك

سورة الملك

الجزء ٢٩ الحزب ٥٧

بسم الله الرحمن الرحيم

تبارك الذي بيده الملك وهو على كل شيء قدير ١ الذي خلق
الموت والحياة ليبلوكم أيكم أحسن عملا وهو العزيز الغفور ٢
الذي خلق سبع سماوات طباقا ما ترى في خلق الرحمن من
تفاوت فارجع البصر هل ترى من فطور ٣ ثم ارجع البصر كرتين
ينقلب إليك البصر خاسئا وهو حسير ٤ ولقد زينا السماء
الدنيا بمصابيح وجعلناها رجوما للشياطين وأعتدنا لهم عذاب
السعير ٥ وللذين كفروا بربهم عذاب جهنم وبئس المصير ٦
إذا ألقوا فيها سمعوا لها شهيقا وهي تفور ٧ تكاد تميز
من الغيظ كلما ألقي فيها فوج سألهم خزنتها ألم يأتكم نذير ٨
قالوا بلى قد جاءنا نذير فكذبنا وقلنا ما نزل الله من شيء إن أنتم
إلا في ضلال كبير ٩ وقالوا لو كنا نسمع أو نعقل ما كنا في أصحاب
السعير ١٠ فاعترفوا بذنبهم فسحقا لأصحاب السعير ١١ إن
الذين يخشون ربهم بالغيب لهم مغفرة وأجر كبير ١٢

٥٦٢

I like to memorise verse by verse, taking things slowly. My criteria for moving on to the next verse is that I have to be able to connect the first verse with the one after it with ease. If I cannot do that, then I will not move on.

So, I would start with the first verse:

تَبَـٰرَكَ ٱلَّذِى بِيَدِهِ ٱلْمُلْكُ وَهُوَ عَلَىٰ كُلِّ شَىْءٍ قَدِيرٌ

I will repeat this verse as many times that I need for it to be stuck in my memory. Some teachers and students like to follow the technique where you read each verse seven times by looking and another seven times without looking. I don't personally think this approach works for me as each verse is completely different. Different in length, different in difficulty and different in tajweed. Therefore, it would be unfair to assume that each verse needs to be repeated seven times for it to be stuck in my brain.

I will repeat the verse as many times as necessary, which can be as little as twice or three times, all the way to twenty to thirty times of repetition. I think that doing it this way is a lot better because you are adjusting based on the verse, you may be able to memorise one verse quickly, and it may be very easy for you. In this case, it would not make sense to repeat it seven times, and instead, that energy could be used on another verse that you are not so strong at.

Once I have finished the first verse, I will recite the second verse:

ٱلَّذِى خَلَقَ ٱلْمَوْتَ وَٱلْحَيَوٰةَ لِيَبْلُوَكُمْ أَيُّكُمْ أَحْسَنُ عَمَلًا ۚ وَهُوَ ٱلْعَزِيزُ ٱلْغَفُورُ

Again, I will repeat it as many times for it to be stored in my memory

Notice what I said just a minute ago. I will not move on to another verse until I can connect it to the one after it. Therefore, I would repeat the first verse and the second verse, and I would have to be able to connect them together with ease to be able to move on to the next verse. If I cannot do that, I will stay at those two verses until I can.

Once I have done that, I will move on to the next verse:

ٱلَّذِى خَلَقَ سَبْعَ سَمَـٰوَٰتٍ طِبَاقًا ۖ مَّا تَرَىٰ فِى خَلْقِ ٱلرَّحْمَـٰنِ مِن تَفَـٰوُتٍ ۖ فَٱرْجِعِ
ٱلْبَصَرَ هَلْ تَرَىٰ مِن فُطُورٍ

Now that we are at the 3rd verse, again, I would repeat as many times as needed, and then I would make sure that I can connect it very well with the second verse. Now is where things will get different. Most people in this instance would continue this pattern until the end of the page; however, this is not a good idea because it means you would only be doing one round of repeating each verse, meaning that by the time you get to the bottom of the page, you would have very likely forgotten the first few verses.

A way that I combat this Is that when I get to the third verse, I will start again from verse number one and read until verse three, making sure that I am reciting with proficiency and connecting the verses well. I am not doing it merely from verse two to verse three only, leaving out verse one.

No, instead, each time I memorise a new verse from the third verse onwards, I start again from verse one and recite up to each new verse that I memorise.

I would then move on to the next verse:

ثُمَّ ٱرْجِعِ ٱلْبَصَرَ كَرَّتَيْنِ يَنقَلِبْ إِلَيْكَ ٱلْبَصَرُ خَاسِئًا وَهُوَ حَسِيرٌ

Again, repeat it as many times as you need for it to be stuck in your memory. Then you would start again from the first verse and read up until the fourth verse, again making sure that you are connecting the verses well.

Notice how I put a lot of emphasis on connecting the verses. This is very important, especially the further you get into your journey, where the surahs will get longer and have a lot more pages.

You will also notice that it will become more and more difficult the longer the verses become. I still, to this day, struggle to connect verses at the end of the page and the start of a fresh page when the surah has many pages. Therefore, you need to take this very seriously.

This is the memorisation method that I personally used myself to memorise the Quran from cover to cover. I would highly advise you to also try it for yourself and see if you like it.

With that said, let's introduce you to a few more Quran memorisation techniques that I am aware of.

Other memorisation techniques

The 3x3 method

The idea with the 3x3 method is that you would recite each verse 3 times before moving on to the next one while you are fixated on the page. Once you have memorised the first verse and repeated it three times, you will move on to the next verse and also repeat that verse 3 times. Once you have repeated it three times, you will go back to the first verse and connect the verses together.

This method is very similar to the method that I used. The only difference is that you have to recite each verse three times before moving on to the next verse. However, with my method, I don't necessarily repeat it three times. It can be more or less.

Another thing to note with this method is that when you get to the end of the page, you will also repeat the page three times. So, you repeat each verse three times, recite the next verse also three times, connect them all and at the end, simply repeat the page 3 times.

This is also a great memorisation method as there is a lot of repetition going on here. Some people would prefer this method as it is more systematic. Some people simply like to follow orders and are organised when things are done like this.

The 20 times method

This method goes as follows. The following is an example for the first page of Surah Al Jummuah. Of course, the number of verses will differ from page to page, so please do bear that in mind:

- Read the first verse twenty times
- Read the second verse twenty times.
- Read the third verse twenty times.
- Read the fourth verse twenty times.
- Read all of the verses from first to fourth twenty times.
- Read the fifth verse twenty times.
- Read the sixth verse twenty times.
- Read the seventh verse twenty times.
- Read the eight verses twenty times.
- Read from verse five to verse eight twenty times.
- Read from the first verse to verse eight 20 times.

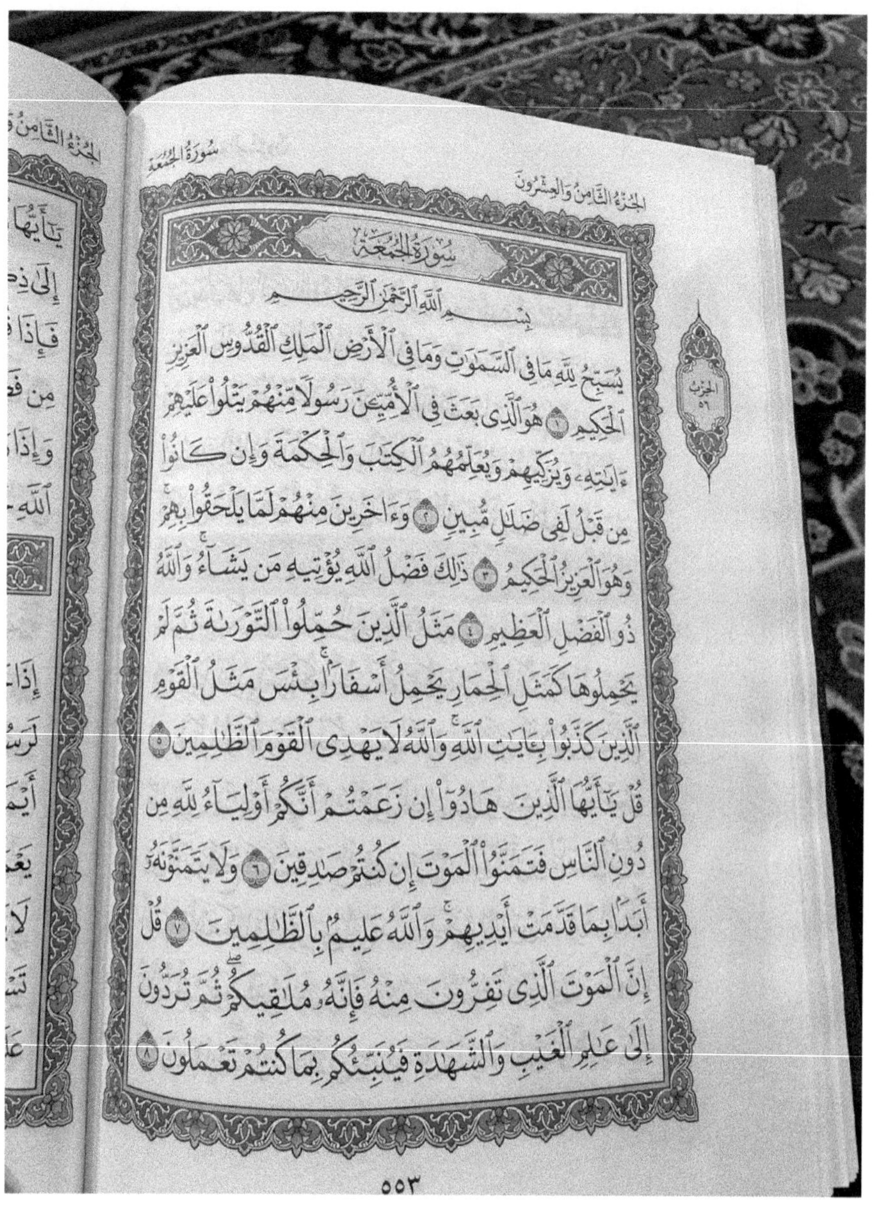

الجزء الثامن والعشرون سورة الجمعة

سورة الجمعة

بسم الله الرحمن الرحيم

الحزب ٥٦

يسبح لله ما في السموت وما في الأرض الملك القدوس العزيز
الحكيم ﴿١﴾ هو الذي بعث في الأميين رسولا منهم يتلوا عليهم
ءايته ويزكيهم ويعلمهم الكتب والحكمة وإن كانوا
من قبل لفي ضلل مبين ﴿٢﴾ وءاخرين منهم لما يلحقوا بهم
وهو العزيز الحكيم ﴿٣﴾ ذلك فضل الله يؤتيه من يشاء والله
ذو الفضل العظيم ﴿٤﴾ مثل الذين حملوا التورىة ثم لم
يحملوها كمثل الحمار يحمل أسفارا بئس مثل القوم
الذين كذبوا بـايت الله والله لا يهدي القوم الظلمين ﴿٥﴾
قل يأيها الذين هادوا إن زعمتم أنكم أولياء لله من
دون الناس فتمنوا الموت إن كنتم صدقين ﴿٦﴾ ولا يتمنونه
أبدا بما قدمت أيديهم والله عليم بالظلمين ﴿٧﴾ قل
إن الموت الذي تفرون منه فإنه ملقيكم ثم تردون
إلى علم الغيب والشهدة فينبئكم بما كنتم تعملون ﴿٨﴾

٥٥٣

Above is the first page of surah Jummuah. Try the above steps on this first page. After you have done this, you will realise that the memory is very strong.

I also highly recommend this method.

Whichever method you choose out of the three, remember that you will have to stay consistent no matter which ones you choose. They say that it takes around 30 days to form a habit, so whichever method you decide to go with, please give it at least 30 days before switching or trying something else.

When you have found something that works well for you, please stick with it.

My final request…

Being a smaller author, reviews help me tremendously!

It would mean the world to me if you could leave a review.

If you liked reading this book and learned a thing or two, please let me know!

It only takes 30 seconds, but it means so much to me!

Thank you, and I can't wait to see your thought.

Jazakhallu Khair.

Conclusion

Thank you for reading my book, and I hope you have benefited tremendously.

This book was written with the intention of motivating the youth to embark on the journey of memorising the Quran. Remember that memorisation is easier the younger you are, and the older you get, the more difficult it will be.

With that said, there are plenty of examples of elderly people that have memorised the Quran, so never think that it is not possible, nor that you are too old to memorise. Some of the best scholars of our time memorised the Quran in their late twenties.

This spiritual journey will be the best journey that you have embarked on in sha Allah. Always ask Allah to make things easier for you.

Lastly, I would like to end this book with the hadith of our beloved prophet SAW, where he said:

احرص على ما ينفعك، واستعن بالله ولا تعجز

"Take care of that which is beneficial for you, keep asking Allah for help and do not refrain from asking."

And remember, the journey with the Quran is a life journey, not a two- or three-year journey.

I ask Allah to make the memorisation of the Quran easy for you and to keep you steadfast in his religion.

Resources

Quran.com. 2022. *Tafsir Surah Al-Muzzammil - 4 - Quran.com.* [online] Available at: <https://quran.com/en/73:4/tafsirs/en-tafsir-maarif-ul-quran> [Accessed 4 August 2022].

Encyclopedia of Translated Prophetic Hadiths. 2022. *Hadith: Whoever does not recite the Qur'an with a melodious voice is not one of us - Encyclopedia of Translated Prophetic Hadiths.* [online] Available at: <https://hadeethenc.com/en/browse/hadith/6276> [Accessed 4 August 2022].

Daily Hadith Online. 2022. *Hadith on Quran: Parents of children who recite Quran given a crown.* [online] Available at: <https://www.abuaminaelias.com/dailyhadithonline/2019/05/12/parents-hafiz-quran-crown/> [Accessed 4 August 2022].

Daily Hadith Online. 2022. *Hadith on Quran: Recite and ascend the levels of Paradise.* [online] Available at: <https://www.abuaminaelias.com/dailyhadithonline/2013/05/16/recite-ascend-paradise/> [Accessed 4 August 2022].

Sunnah.com. 2022. *Riyad as-Salihin 387 - The Book of Miscellany - Sunnah.com - Sayings and Teachings of Prophet Muhammad.* [online] Available at: <https://sunnah.com/riyadussalihin:387> [Accessed 4 August 2022].

Medium. 2022. *10 Unbelievable Health Benefits of Memorising the Qur'ān.* [online] Available at: <https://medium.com/how-to-memorise-the-quran/10-unbelievable-health-benefits-of-memorising-the-qur%C4%81n-77cd3fe31c2b> [Accessed 4 August 2022].

Quran.com. 2022. *Surah An-Nahl - 1-128 - Quran.com.* [online] Available at: <https://quran.com/en/an-nahl> [Accessed 4 August 2022].

www.ingramcontent.com/pod-product-compliance
Ingram Content Group UK Ltd.
Pitfield, Milton Keynes, MK11 3LW, UK
UKHW022015190726
13853UKWH00005B/1956

9 788286 756477